Elements of Quality:
The Sloan-C™ Framework

by Janet C. Moore

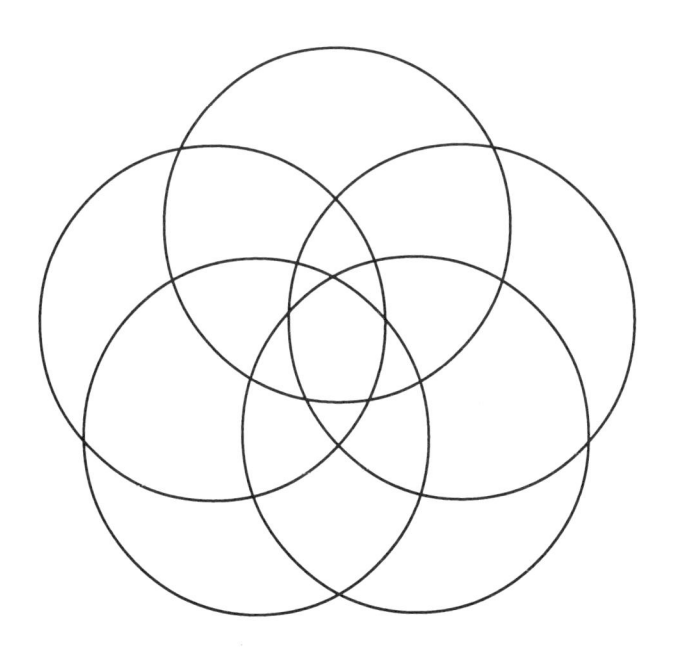

THE SLOAN CONSORTIUM
A Consortium of Institutions and Organizations
Committed to Quality Online Education

This book contains information obtained from authentic and highly regarded sources. Reprinted material is quoted with permission, and sources are indicated. A wide variety of references are listed. Reasonable efforts have been made to publish reliable data and information, but the author and the publishers cannot assume responsibility for the validity of all materials or for the consequences of their use.

Neither this book nor any part may be reproduced or transmitted in any form or by any means, electronic or mechanical, including photocopying, microfilming, scanning, and recording, or by any information storage or retrieval system, without prior permission in writing from the publisher.

The consent of Sloan-C™ and the Sloan Center for OnLine Education (SCOLE) does not extend to copying for general distribution, for promotion, for creating new works, or for resale. Specific permission must be obtained in writing from SCOLE for such copying. Direct all inquiries to SCOLE, at 1735 Great Plain Avenue, Needham, MA 02492-1245, or to publisher@sloan-c.org.

Copyright ©2002 by Sloan-C™
All rights reserved. Published 2002
Printed in the United States of America
0 9 8 7 6 5 4 3 2 1

International Standard Book Number 0-9677741-3-6

Elements of Quality: The Sloan-C™ Framework
Pillar Reference Manual

Elements of Quality: The Sloan-C™ Framework is the collected wisdom of practitioners who improve the quality of learning in online programs. This *Pillar Reference Manual* shows how schools have applied the five pillars of quality—learning effectiveness, cost effectiveness, access, faculty satisfaction, and student satisfaction—in a flexible quality framework that can be used in the full range of academic contexts.

Thanks to the Alfred P. Sloan Foundation for its generous support of online learning; to the scholars whose research continues to improve the quality of learning; and to the Sloan Center for OnLine Education for sharing a wealth of resources in the *Journal of Asynchronous Learning Networks* and in the annual Sloan-C™ volumes on quality.

This work is supported by the Alfred P. Sloan Foundation.

SCOLE
Sloan Center for OnLine Education
at Olin and Babson Colleges

Sloan-C has its administrative home at the Sloan Center for OnLine Education (SCOLE) at Olin and Babson Colleges. SCOLE has been established as a center that spans the two campus of Olin College and Babson College. SCOLE's purpose is to support the activities of the Sloan Consortium, a consortium of higher-education providers sharing the common bonds of understanding, supporting and delivering education via asynchronous learning networks (ALNs). With the mission of providing learning to anyone anywhere, SCOLE seeks to provide new levels of learning capability to people seeking higher and continuing education. For more information about SCOLE, visit www.scole.olin-babson.org.

For more information about Olin and Babson Colleges, visit www.olin.edu and www.babson.edu.

Franklin W. Olin College of Engineering

BABSON COLLEGE

Contents

I. Introduction: Being Proactive 1

II. The Pillars 7
    A. Learning Effectiveness: Begin with the End in Mind 7
        1. Good Practice: Interaction, Timeliness, Support 8
        2. Personalizing Instruction 10
        3. People Networks, Learning Community 12
        4. Designing Legacies 16
    B. Cost Effectiveness: Put First Things First 20
        1. Benefits: Teaching, Learning, Discovery, Growth 21
        2. New Costs: Infrastructure, Training, Rewards 23
        3. Methods and Resources: Re-thinking and Shifting 23
    C. Access: Think Win/Win 26
        1. Scaffolding: Infrastructure and Course Management 26
        2. Learning Support Services 30
        3. The Future of Access: Mind to Mind 32
    D. Faculty Satisfaction: Seek First to Understand 33
        1. Faculty Benefits: Diversity, Reach, Interdisciplinarity 34
        2. Faculty Resistance: Time, Authority, Recognition 36
        3. Challenges: Wise Design 39
    E. Student Satisfaction: Synergize 42
        1. What Learners Want 43
        2. Why Do Learners Drop Out? 44
        3. Immeasurable Benefits 47

III. The Quality Framework: Sharpen the Saw 53

Appendix A: Pillar Reference Quick Guide 69
    Learning Effectiveness 69
    Cost Effectiveness 69
    Access 69
    Faculty Satisfaction 70
    Student Satisfaction 70

Appendix B: Effective Practices 71

Appendix C: References (alphabetized) 77

Appendix D: References (by section) 87

Index 99

Figures

Figure 1: Matrix for Community Building 14
Figure 2: Curriculum Design 16
Figure 3: Legacy Cycle 18
Figure 4: Online Services 31
Figure 5: Analysis of Time Shifts in Faculty Activities 39
Figure 6: Interdependency of Pillars 55

Tables

Table 1: Brief Version of the Quality Framework 3
Table 2: eArmyU's Design Specifications for CMSs 27
Table 3: Learning Effectiveness 60
Table 4: Cost Effectiveness 62
Table 5: Access 64
Table 6: Faculty Satisfaction 66
Table 7: Student Satisfaction 67
Table 8: Learning Effectiveness Practices 72
Table 9: Cost Effectiveness Practices 73
Table 10: Access Practices 74
Table 11: Faculty Satisfaction Practices 75
Table 12: Student Satisfaction Practices 76

I. Introduction:*
Being Proactive

The story of the five pillars of quality in education begins with the vision of a future in which anyone anywhere at any time has access to learning as an ordinary part of everyday life [1]. How close are we to realizing this vision?

We can trace our early twenty-first ideas about quality in learning to the earliest teachers who questioned how people learn. For Plato, quality is an ineffable ideal, matter is corrupt, and our experience is merely a poor approximation of perfection; Plato's learning is a deductive process of stripping away sensory illusions to recall the good, the true and the beautiful. But for Aristotle, quality is innate in matter, and things are good when they realize their purpose; learning is the inductive discovery of purpose and its development. For both Plato and Aristotle, only a very few people would be capable of the abstract thinking that learning requires. When Philip of Macedonia employed Aristotle to teach his son Alexander to be great, he purchased the best education money could buy—one-to-one personalized instruction in all the arts and sciences of being, knowing and doing. Only the few, with birthrights of wealth or good fortune, could afford formal affiliation with the masters. Universities grew up around the apprentice-master paradigm, even as printing widened access to learning far beyond the one-to-one ideal.

Today, access to formal learning is expanding in ways the ancients or even those in the recent past could not have imagined. Even as recently as a decade ago, when the first programs were going online, mostly clones of text-based courses in which notes and assignments were listed for "off-campus learners [who] worked mainly in isolation, with only occasional contact with instructors and peers" [2], most educators would not have expected the current exponential growth in demand for online learning. Yet, some, skilled in the arts of possibility, could see that online learning would require proactive measures to ensure that the quality of learning outside the classroom would be at least equivalent to learning inside it.

In 1997, the director of the Sloan Foundation Program for Learning Outside the Classroom articulated a few holistic principles to guide the development of quality in the burgeoning industry of online learning. Frank Mayadas explained that any learner who engages in online education should have, at a minimum, an education that represents the quality of the provider's overall

---

*The section titles of this book allude to Steven R. Covey's *Seven Habits of Highly Effective People*. New York: Simon and Schuster, 1990. The principles for building quality align with Covey's principles for building character.

institutional quality. Like traditional students, online learners should have interaction with an instructor who is available outside the classroom and interaction with classmates in learning experiences that include equivalent course material and the same academic standards. These special qualifications for online learning are known as asynchronous learning networks (ALNs). Asynchronous learning networks, interactive networks of people connected with technology, enable participation in learning activities according to diverse schedules [3]. Mayadas emphasizes a critically important insight for quality: "We can think of every person on the network as both a user and a resource" [2]. People know the principles that emerged from this perspective on the quality of online learning as the five pillars of asynchronous learning networks (ALN):

- Learning Effectiveness
- Cost Effectiveness
- Access
- Faculty Satisfaction
- Student Satisfaction

The five pillars compose an easily remembered heuristic frame for the profound interdependence of common goals. Each pillar names a value, a purpose, and an outcome, and each suggests processes to achieve the goal of making "education a part of everyday life, accessible and affordable for anyone, anywhere, at any time, in a wide variety of disciplines" [4]. Any learning organization demonstrates its quality through its answers to these questions:

- **Learning Effectiveness**: What has the institution learned about how well learning takes place?
- **Cost Effectiveness**: Is there sufficient motivation for the institution to scale up online education?
- **Access**: To what extent has the interactive model increased access to quality education, beyond what would have been possible through the established method of distributing self-learning materials?
- **Faculty Satisfaction**: What has the institution learned about how easy (difficult) it is for faculty to develop and teach online courses?
- **Student Satisfaction**: What has been learned about overall satisfaction of enrolled students? [5]

It is important, Mayadas reminds everyone, to measure outcomes in each of these interdependent areas, because costs affect the quality of access to learning. Thus, the Sloan Foundation has encouraged metrics-based, empirical research and the sharing of effective practices among accredited colleges and universities that subscribe to the five pillars. More than two hundred of these institutions have joined together to form the Sloan Consortium (Sloan-C™). Through the *Journal of Asynchronous Learning Networks* and annual volumes of *Online Education,* educators have provided the empirical and applied research that demonstrates the effectiveness of the five pillars and the quality framework this manual introduces. Table 1, a brief version of the framework, illustrates how metrics can show progress toward representative goals (see Chapter 3, "The Quality Framework," for a longer version of the framework).

Table 1: Brief Version of the Quality Framework

Learning Effectiveness			
Goal	Process/Practice	Metric	Progess Indexes
The quality of learning online is demonstrated to be at least as good as the quality the institution provides in traditional programs.	Academic integrity and control reside with faculty in the same way as in traditional programs at the provider institution.	Faculty perception surveys or sampled interviews compare learning effectiveness in delivery modes. Learner/graduate/employer focus groups or interviews measure learning gains.	Faculty report online learning is equivalent or better. Direct assessment of student learning is equivalent or better.

Cost Effectiveness			
Goal	Process/Practice	Metric	Progess Indexes
The institution continuously improves services while reducing costs.	The institution demonstrates financial and technical commitment to its online programs. Tuition rates provide a fair return to institution and best value to learners at the same time.	Institutional stakeholders show support for participation in online education. Effective practices are identified.	The institution sustains the program, expands and scales upward as desired, strengthens and disseminates its mission and core values through online education.

Pillar Reference Manual

Cost Effectiveness *continued*			
Goal	Process/Practice	Metric	Progess Indexes
	Tuition rates are equivalent or less than on-campus tuition.		

Access			
Goal	Process/Practice	Metric	Progess Indexes
All learners who wish to learn online can access learning in a wide array of programs and courses.	Program entry processes inform learners of opportunities, and ensure that qualified, motivated learners have reliable access. Integrated support services are available online to learners.	Administrative and technical infrastructure provides access to all prospective and enrolled learners Quality metrics for information dissemination, learning resources delivery, and tutoring services.	Qualitative indicators show continuous improvement in growth and effectiveness rates.

Faculty Satisfaction			
Goal	Process/Practice	Metric	Progess Indexes
Faculty are pleased with teaching online, citing appreciation and happiness.	Processes ensure faculty participation in matters particular to online education (e.g., governance, intellectual property, royalty sharing, etc.). Processes ensure adequate support for faculty in course preparation and course delivery.	Repeat teaching of online courses by individual faculty indicates approval. Addition of new faculty shows growing endorsement.	Data from post-course surveys show continuous improvement: At least 90% of faculty believes the overall online teaching/learning experience is positive. Willingness/desire to teach additional courses in the program: 80% positive.

I. Introduction

Student Satisfaction			
Goal	Process/Practice	Metric	Progress Indexes
Students are pleased with their experiences in learning online, including interaction with instructors and peers, learning outcomes that match expectations, services, and orientation.	Faculty/learner interaction is timely and substantive. Adequate and fair systems assess course learning objectives; results are used for improving learning.	Metrics show growing satisfaction: Surveys (see above) and/or interviews. Alumni surveys, referrals, testimonials. Outcomes measures. Focus groups. Faculty/Mentor/- Advisor perceptions.	Satisfaction measures show continuously increasing improvement. Institutional surveys, interviews, or other metrics show satisfaction levels are equivalent to or better than those of other delivery modes for the institution.

Although the precepts of continuous quality improvement (CQI) or total quality management (TQM) are well known—customer satisfaction, employee and supplier satisfaction, and continuous improvement of product, process, and purpose based on input from stakeholders—some educational institutions have been slow to adopt CQI, partly because "some of the key benefits of education are simply not immediately measurable as outcomes, economic or otherwise," and partly because time-honored faculty and research-centered focuses tended to segregate business considerations from academic ones [6]. But the advent of online learning and the pedagogy that is evolving with technology make CQI clearly beneficial to higher education. In the business of education—to improve learning while achieving capacity enrollment—CQI helps people to set goals, identify resources and strategies, and measure progress towards the institution's ideal vision of its distinctive purpose. Thus, in the quality framework, the goals of each of the five pillars are developed in CQI terms for measuring continuously improving learning, affordability, access, and faculty and student satisfaction— interactive components that focus on improving people networks, practices, achievement and growth.

In little more than a decade, online learning has become a major growth industry, and educational associations have established guidelines for assuring quality. Guidelines from these organizations contribute to an understanding of the five pillars from a variety of perspectives that share common goals. Organizations that have created guidelines for quality online education include:

- American Council of Education: http://www.acenet.edu/calec/dist_learning/dl_orgCommitment.html
- American Distance Education Consortium: http://www.adec.edu
- Institute for Higher Education/NEA Benchmarks: http://www.ihep.com/PR17.html
- Southern Regional Electronic Campus *Principles of Good Practice*: http://www.electroniccampus.org/student/srecinfo/publications/principles.asp
- Western Cooperative for Educational Telecommunications' *Principles of Good Practice for Electronically Offered Academic Degree and Certificate Programs*: http://www.wiche.edu/telecom/projects/balancing/principles.htm
- The Sloan Consortium: http://www.sloan-c.org/catalog/alncriteria.htm

With few exceptions, the recommendations of the groups listed above are useful for specifically *asynchronous* online programs that emphasize interaction, and most of the guidelines, contribute at least implicitly to the heuristic function of the quality framework. As institutions make decisions about the best ways to improve quality, the pillars and the framework are intended to make visible multiple simultaneous perspectives about value, priorities, tradeoffs, gap analyses, capacity management and more. "Quality" as defined in this manual is the dynamic, relational character each institution creates according to its mission and the people who embody it.

II. The Pillars

A. Learning Effectiveness: Begin with the End in Mind

ALN research has sufficiently demonstrated that learning online is as effective as learning in other modes, according to Hiltz and colleagues who analyzed 19 empirical studies that compare online learning with face-to-face learning [7]. Not only does online learning compare favorably, Hiltz points out that it has the potential to enable schools to do things not possible before, including customizing courses for special populations, using new communications tools, reducing distinctions between nearby and distant learners, and using new resources and teaching methods. Online learning can change the nature of courses, programs, departments, institutions, assessment and evaluation; it creates long-term impacts on learners of diverse abilities, and the reputation of the institution [8]. As the medium shapes the message, it also shapes its users [9]. Thus, Chris Dede summarizes the challenges that are before us:

> We're facing the biggest gap between yesterday's workplace and tomorrow's that any group of educators has faced since the dawn of the Industrial Revolution a couple of centuries ago. And yet the very technologies that are creating this challenge are also providing an opportunity to meet it. In contrast to simply automating presentation, there's a lot that interactive learning technologies can do to address more powerful forms of pedagogy—based on learning by doing, collaborative learning, and mentoring via apprenticeships [10].

Time-honored traditional paradigms for learning frame teaching and learning in relationships of sage/disciple, master/apprentice, professor/pupil, teacher/learner; these relationships are hierarchical and have occasionally been interpreted as a sort of parent/child relationship, as in the image of the university as an *alma mater*. More recently, we characterize the educational relationship as "novice/expert"—to respectfully acknowledge that a novice in one context may be an expert in another. Thus, Dede and others talk about teachers and learners online engaging in more collaborative relationships. Nevertheless, many people prefer independent learning, and many worthy examples of self-taught prodigies like Abraham Lincoln and Srinivasa Ramanujan, or like the supposed "dunces" Thomas Aquinas and Albert Einstein, demonstrate that learning is not only social but is also inherently individuated. Yet the social promise of online learning suggests, as John Seely Brown points out, that "growing up digital" can change "work, education, and the ways people learn." As the push and pull medium of online learning opens formal education to greater informal exchange among discovery-based learning communities, the Internet may be as transformative of social practices as electricity. In fact, says Brown:

> The real literacy of tomorrow entails the ability to be your own personal reference librarian—to know how to navigate through confusing, complex information spaces and feel comfortable doing so. "Navigation" may well be the main form of literacy for the 21st century [11].

1. Good Practice: Interaction, Timeliness, Support

Research on learning effectiveness as summarized in Chickering and Gamson's "Seven Principles for Good Practice in Undergraduate Education," first published by the American Association for Higher Education in 1987, was updated for online learning based on an international 1994 workgroup [12]. Still, each of the seven principles is a feature of learning effectiveness in any mode:

1. Good practice encourages contacts between students and faculty.
2. Good practice develops reciprocity and cooperation among students.
3. Good practice uses active learning techniques.
4. Good practice gives prompt feedback.
5. Good practice emphasizes time on task.
6. Good practice communicates high expectations.
7. Good practice respects diverse talents and ways of learning.

In the 1994 commentary on the ways technology influences practices, Chickering and Ehrmann write: "The biggest success in this realm has been that of time-delayed (asynchronous) communication . . . . Total communication increases and, for many students, the result seems more intimate, protected, and convenient than the more intimidating demands of face-to-face communication with faculty" [12]. In fact, according to studies at the University of Central Florida [13], the New Jersey Institute of Technology [14], and the State University of New York Learning Network (SLN) [15] the quality of online communication, especially collaborative interaction, is the single most important factor in learning effectiveness, in faculty satisfaction, and in student satisfaction.

In 2002, in *Effectiveness and Efficiency in Higher Education for Adults*, Keeton, Scheckley, and Krecji-Griggs have adapted and revised the 7

II. The Pillars

principles according to a survey of twenty years of teaching practices, basing their 8 principles on the practices they find to have the greatest impact on learning gains:

1. Make learning goals and one or more paths to them clear.
2. Use deliberate practice and provide prompt constructive feedback.
3. Provide an optimal balance of challenge and support that is tailored to the individual students' readiness and potential.
4. Broaden the learners' experience of the subject matter.
5. Elicit active and critical reflection by learners on their growing experience base.
6. Link inquiries to genuine problems or issues of high interest to the learners to enhance motivation and accelerate their learning.
7. Develop learners' effectiveness as learners early in their education.
8. Create an institutional environment that supports and encourages inquiry.

For each of the principles, numerous strategies are available; and in the first phase of their project, Keeton, Scheckley and Krecji-Griggs have designed an Instructional Practices Inventory to share the strategies that the most effective teachers use for online teaching [16]. In another ongoing study that uses the principles of good practice as metrics, the SUNY Learning Network reports benchmarks drawn from the responses of 935 students:

- 70% of students reported very high quality interaction with classmates.
- 71% reported spending more time studying as a result of the increased access afforded by the online format.
- 73% reported high levels of interaction with classmates.
- 75% reported high levels of interaction with faculty.
- 78% reported very high quality interaction with instructors.
- 83% reported that the online format helped them improve their ability to communicate effectively in writing.
- 85% reported very prompt feedback.
- 87% reported that they had received high quality, constructive feedback.
- 87% reported being satisfied or very satisfied with their courses.
- 90% report learning a great deal.
- 90% reported that the instructor provided clear expectations of how students could succeed in the course.
- 93.4% reported active participation in their online classes.

- 94% reported being satisfied or very satisfied with SLN service.
- 97% reported satisfaction with the SLN Helpdesk.
- Students were twice as likely to report more active participation in online discussion than in classroom.
- Students were twice as likely to report asking for clarification online than in the classroom.
- The "busiest" students report highest satisfaction with online learning, according to reports from students who learn online because of distance or lack of transportation, because of conflict with personal schedule, because the course is not offered on campus, because of family responsibilities or because of interest in technology and the internet [17].

Clearly, indicators show that equivalent learning occurs online and that good pedagogy improves learning; moreover, some indicators show that online learning offers new kinds of access that embrace personal preference and learning style. Thus, Kaliym Islam notes that today's learners, many of whom are cybernatives, ask of online learning: "WIIFM or what's in it for me?" Learners want to take control of their own learning experiences using their own set patterns of learning. They "are not beginners but are in a continual state of growth" bringing with them "a package of experiences and values, each one unique," with intentions, expectations about learning, and competing interests [18].

2. Personalizing Instruction

The Pew Center for Academic Transformation monograph "Innovations in Online Learning: Moving Beyond No Significant Difference" asserts that personalizing instruction with the aid of technology offers powerful opportunities for learning and pedagogical strategies. From traditional practices like the cycle of lecturing, reading, and testing, online programs are moving to more active learning by assessing individual knowledge and learning styles, creating interactive learning materials and activities, building in instantaneous feedback, and using collaboration [19]. Key to the success of active learning according to many practitioners is the opportunity to personalize learning in innovative ways through approaches that emphasize the uniqueness of individual learners and employ authentic, agentive course work. The University of Phoenix, for example, welcomes students by including their names on the screens they access, and collects learners' personal information to maintain individualized relationships with them and to personalize feedback on their work in progress [20]; for visual learners, Lanny Arvan at the University of Illinois designs and shares Excel models to help people see quantitative concepts with animations of graphs and numerical data [21]; Ed Kashy and Michael Thoennessen at Michigan State University helped design CAPA, a quizzer, randomizer, grader, and manager that helps students

II. The Pillars

identify their own errors and correct individualized problems [22]; Prisoner's Dilemma interactive problem-solving games at Bryn Mawr's Serendip develop individual thinking about collaboration and competition [23]; at the University of Amherst dilemma games engage learners in dispute resolution [24]; at Penn State, David DiBiase inaugurated "student learning e-portfolios" so students can more actively plan their own educational goals, share examples of their work with potential employers, master transferable information technology skills, demonstrate knowledge gained beyond the classroom, and demonstrate authentic evidence of learning outcomes [25]; at Pepperdine, student teacher Bill Moseley announced his class project—an analysis of the benefits of personalized, active learning—with an online movie trailer that leads to his final paper, a PowerPoint presentation, and a webliography of education groups dedicated to active learning at all levels [26].

To further personalize learning, courses are developed to provide offline learning activities at home, at work, and in local communities that can be shared online with classmates around the globe, enabling learners to discover more about their own cultures while they learn about others. As learners work at home with their families, or among coworkers, or in their local schools and communities, the web of learning expands to affect many other lives. Thus, online learning is enhanced by attention to the processes of knowing that are based on individual prior knowledge, skills, beliefs, and concepts that significantly affect the individual ways in which people learn, notice, remember, reason, solve problems, and acquire new knowledge [27]. In his search for ways to make online learning more flexible, Moseley emphasizes some basic tenets that can help realize the potential of online learning:

> Students are not alike. They don't learn the same. They don't react the same. They don't think they same. Tell any teacher in the world any of these common sense statements, and you are likely to hear the word "duh" somewhere in their response . . . . Learning is a social thing. It's also a personal thing. The key to effective teaching online lies in the instructor's ability to make social and personal connections to students in the course and between the students in the course. Longer-term retention requires a personal connection to that which is learned [26].

Institutions can extend personal connection by designing curricula that incorporate features that reach across courses and disciplines, replicating and expanding learning modules as learners progress to higher level thinking and applications, enabling learners to revisit concepts as sophistication increases, using tests and self-tests more for learning than for grading, enabling more time on task and more effective time engaged in relevant learning challenges and problem solving, all the while awakening learners to the consciousness of how they themselves learn.

3. People Networks, Learning Community

What is the best use of online learning in an information society? What do today's learners need? In answer, Gary Miller, Associate Vice President for Distance Education and Executive Director of Penn State's World Campus, offers these considerations:

> The question is about what society needs . . . . When we talk about online learning, we tend to use the campus and the traditional curriculum as our reference points. I say that online learning reflects not only a new technological capability but also a new kind of social dynamic. It does not exist in isolation. Our students live in an information society where it is very difficult to sort out facts from fiction, truth from bias, etc. What do these students need from a university education in order to be successful in the professions and effective as citizens? They don't need to be given information—that is everywhere—they need to be given the skills to be critical users of information. That is why active, collaborative, inquiry-oriented approaches are so vital—they develop our ability to be critical users of information. This is as much a core skill in an information society as public speaking was in the 19th century. As our field expands and matures, we will want . . . online learning as both a social good and an individual good. So far, the social good argument has been about access. In the future, the social good should also include the unique pedagogy that is enabled by online learning [28].

The unique features of online pedagogy—the quality of interaction and the ease with which discussions and projects can be expanded, applied, archived and revisited—are as transformative to education in the 21st century as were the invention of writing that worried Plato in the 4th century BC, and the invention of the printing press that worried clerics in the 15th century; perhaps, some say, as transformative as electricity. Although we cannot foresee the discoveries greater access to learning will bring, we know too much about the consequences of ignorance, and we believe that learning is vital to the quality of being human.

II. The Pillars

Defining a constructive, virtual learning environment as one that enables learners "to perceive the environment, assess situations and performance, perform actions and proceed through experiences and lessons that will allow them to perform better with more experience on repetition of the same task in similar circumstances," Pimentel describes features designed to enable learners to construct knowledge from experience "to make use of and include examples, observations, experiences, situations, rules, concepts, and techniques in a continuous (e.g., day-by-day or week-by-week), permanent (i.e., committing knowledge into memory) fashion to improve the performance of the execution of tasks" [29]. In an exemplary, detailed examination of the communication behaviors that support learning, Swan describes four kinds of interaction—learners' interactions with content, with instructor, with classmates, and with interface. An equilibrium model of social presence explains the ability of learners to project themselves socially and emotionally in a community of inquiry. Social presence correlates significantly with perceived learning. Thus, Swan advises course designers and instructors to "value course discussions, model and support the development of social presence within courses, and work to build and sustain interactive communities of inquiry in online courses" [30]. As pillar editor for Sloan-C™ effective practices in learning effectiveness, Swan adds "vicarious interaction," or "learning by lurking," as a fifth kind of interaction with which people learn by observing and actively processing interaction among others. Among the most debatable issues about interactions, says Swan, is whether or not peer-to-peer interaction actually contributes to learning:

> In part, the debate rests on what one accepts as learning. Clearly, discussion in online courses is divergent rather than convergent. Those who believe in that thinking and learning are convergent believe that very little is learned in online discussion, although they may believe that it motivates learning in other areas of a course. On the other hand, those who believe that the divergent thinking that considers multiple perspectives is also important find that a good deal of learning goes on in online discussion. Another facet of this debate concerns the efficacy of collaborative learning online. Some researchers have found it remarkably unsuccessful, while others see it as an optimal online pedagogy [31].

Still, the prospect of widening communities of inquiry is among the most exciting promises of online learning. How do these learning communities develop? Campos, Laferrière, and Harasim examine more than one hundred networked classrooms to illustrate the most effective means of collaboration for enabling learners to actively participate with each other in achieving learning goals [32]. Blum shows how online environments that integrate gender-related styles can improve learning access and effectiveness; Blum exposes barriers to participation and community building, including institutional, situational, and dispositional barriers [33]. To find the ways instructors keep discussions productive, Bart Beaudin enlisted 135 online instructors to evaluate techniques for staying on topic [34]; and Murray Turoff details effective ways to design and manage interactive discussions in large classes [35]. With insightful metrics about student access times and frequencies, Steve Andriole advocates "requirements driven" design to deliver ALN to full advantage in achieving and evaluating course outcomes [36]. Joan Taylor chronicles the development of writing skills in a class of writing teachers led by renowned Writing Across the Curriculum expert Don Murray in the National Writing Project [37]. Ruth Brown details the formation of community in online classes, showing how veteran students help novice students build community. Brown's graphic, below, illustrates the stages of community building [38]:

Figure 1: Matrix for Community Building

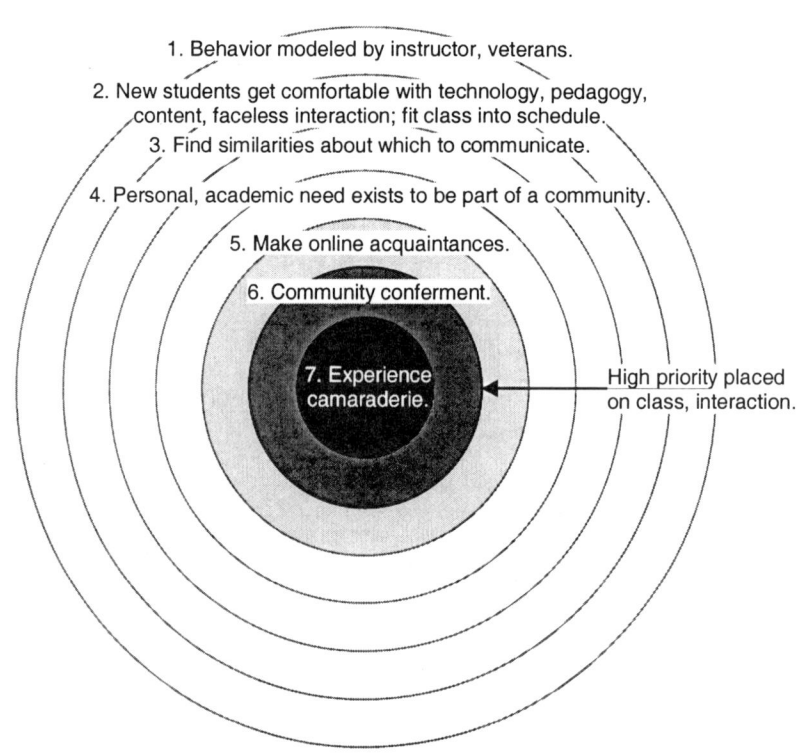

1. Behavior modeled by instructor, veterans.
2. New students get comfortable with technology, pedagogy, content, faceless interaction; fit class into schedule.
3. Find similarities about which to communicate.
4. Personal, academic need exists to be part of a community.
5. Make online acquaintances.
6. Community conferment.
7. Experience camaraderie.

High priority placed on class, interaction.

Darker shades of gray indicate higher levels of:
- Engagement in class and dialog
- Feelings of belonging to a community

Learners report that they like the challenge of engaging with multiple perspectives and having time for the kind of deep reflection that encourages effective communication:

> Being a shy person I am able to think questions and answers through before I respond. In a regular classroom setting I often don't get my question out before we are on to another topic.... There was very prompt response to discussion threads and test and assignment evaluations. Responses to comments were made within a day in most cases. This encouraged students to discuss with the instructor and other students on a regular basis. It felt like the course was alive; and help was there when you needed it [17].

Indeed, Vandergrift asserts that community means that "even if the infrastructure remains basically the same, the people, the environment, and the situations that bring the structure to life come together in new configurations as [learners] find, shape and create new meanings. Such is the richness of educational possibilities." To engage community participation most fully, Vandergrift advocates that teachers use "restrained presence," being present but refraining from the traditional teaching role whenever possible, to bridge transactional distance among learners [39].

Likewise, Rovai finds that effective online learning communities must be based on trust, including:

> Feelings of similarity of needs, recognition of the importance of learning, connectedness, friendship, thinking critically, safety, acceptance, group identity, and absence of confusion.... Trust consists of two dimensions: credibility and benevolence. The first dimension, credibility, is an expectation that the word or written statements of other learners in the community can be relied on. The second dimension, benevolence, is the extent to which learners are genuinely interested in the welfare of other members of the community and are motivated to assist others in their learning. With trust comes the likelihood of candor—that members will feel safe and expose gaps in their learning and feel that other members of the community will respond in supportive ways [40].

4. Designing Legacies

For all learning styles, whether the preferred pedagogical approach is behaviorist, cognitive, or constructivist [41], the design of online courses benefits from including authentic, agentive, active learning that enables learners to perform what they are learning, to work in teams, to engage in substantive discussion, to revisit earlier course modules to retrace learning paths and discover new applications as understanding grows, and to present or publish work for peer review [42]. A central feature of courses designed for learning effectiveness, according to Staley and MacKenzie, are activities that enable students to "'break free' from the computer and perform some tasks in very applied situations, for example, the workplace, laboratory or studio." Figure 2 is their useful map of curriculum design concepts [43]:

Figure 2: Curriculum Design

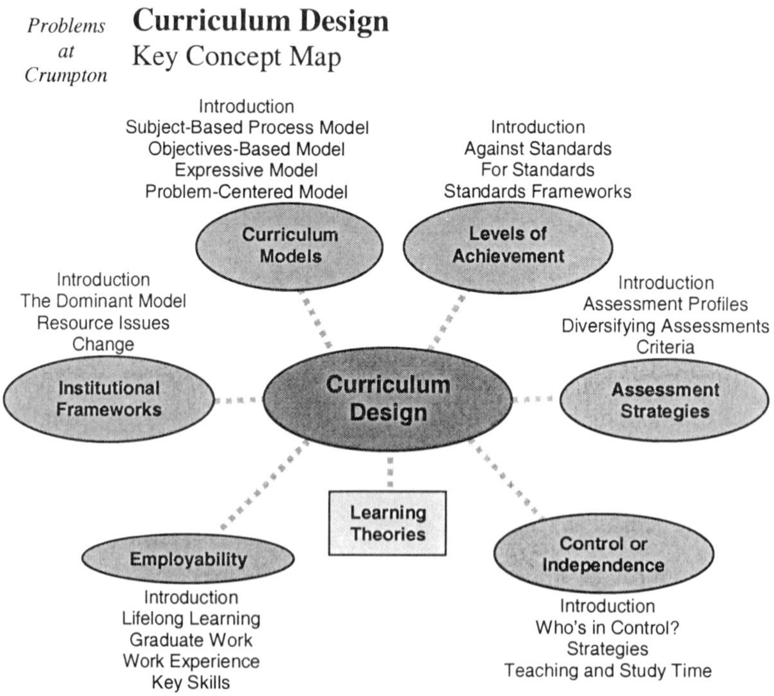

Problems at Crumpton

Curriculum Design
Key Concept Map

Introduction
Subject-Based Process Model
Objectives-Based Model
Expressive Model
Problem-Centered Model

Introduction
Against Standards
For Standards
Standards Frameworks

Curriculum Models

Levels of Achievement

Introduction
The Dominant Model
Resource Issues
Change

Introduction
Assessment Profiles
Diversifying Assessments
Criteria

Institutional Frameworks

Curriculum Design

Assessment Strategies

Learning Theories

Employability

Control or Independence

Introduction
Lifelong Learning
Graduate Work
Work Experience
Key Skills

Introduction
Who's in Control?
Strategies
Teaching and Study Time

II. The Pillars

Crumpton's Curriculum Design concept map [44] illustrates how effective design involves resources inside and outside of the institution, engaging the perspectives of many constituents. Likewise aiming to use the experience of learners, teachers and designers, SUNY Learning Networks has established a legacy through its comprehensive training of hundred of faculty, and recommends specific tips for design. An effective, well-designed, online course has:

- Comprehensive orientation and syllabus documents explicit expectations
- Consistent and complete course chunks/module structure
- Redundant and consistent instructional cues and detailed explanations
- Meaningful and consistent course section and document titles to organize and convey information about the activities, content, and structure of course
- A detailed orientation for each course module
- Detailed instructions for each learning activity, i.e., expectation, timeframe, navigation, etc.
- Course information that is accessible and redundant
- Ample opportunities for interaction with the instructor and with others in the course
- Opportunities to engage and interact with the content actively directed-learning activities

Specific examples of some of the course design recommendations are to:

- Create a non-graded ice-breaking activity in the first module of the course. Using the mechanisms for conducting an online discussion in your course, ask students why they took the course. This will help everyone get to know each other. It provides an opportunity to practice and model a good online discussion, and students who enroll late or have technical difficulties will not be so far behind.
- Encourage a sense of class community and build opportunities for interaction with the instructor and with other students in the course.
- Consider using a self-test the first week of class as a comprehension check on the orientation and syllabus documents for your course. This can make sure that students read that information and eliminate questions later on in the course. It also introduces the testing capability to students in a less threatening way.
- Create navigational instructions that explicitly tell students where to go next and what to do. Do not assume students will know

where to go and what to do next, or for example, what is meant by "discussion."
- Long documents can be broken up into several shorter documents. A good rule of thumb is to not exceed four to five screens for scrolling. On long documents the instructor can inform the student at the top of the page, "You may want to print this out for easier reading."
- Use heads, subheads, hypertext, and a document hierarchy to break up long paragraphs. But do not break them up so much that it affects the flow or meaning.
- Put important information at the beginning of a document.
- Use short descriptive titles for document subjects and module names. Long titles do not fit well on the screen and they lose their purpose. Indicate the type of assignment, due dates, or time frames in the subject lines or module names and use them consistently throughout your course.
- Use directives, first person, and a friendly conversational tone. This personalizes the course for the student.
- Do not overuse hypertext to link your course pages or to link to other Web sites.
- Proofread and spell check work.
- Consider creating a prepared welcome mail message that can be forwarded to students as they appear in the course over the course of the first week.
- Consider sending out an introductory letter to students that specifies the first offline reading assignments for the first couple of weeks. If they have technical problems they can do the initial reading, know what they should be preparing, and not be so far behind when they finally get online. Instructors may also want to design the activities in their course for the first couple of weeks with this in mind [17].

Figure 3: Legacy Cycle™

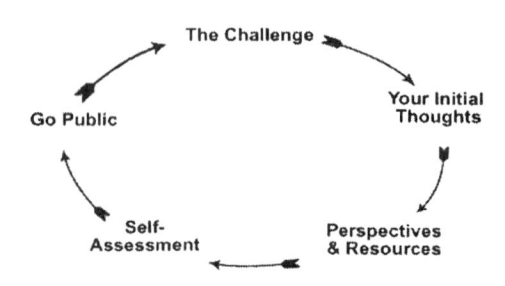

II. The Pillars

The Legacy Cycle™ in Figure 3 shows a constructive cycle of student learning activity that commences with a challenge, progresses to team-oriented collection of ideas, secures materials, and does research [27]. Reflection is then followed by presentation. The cycle can continue and/or leave a legacy of knowledge for students that follow. In this model, effective learning is social, collaborative, flexible, personalized, active, and reflective.

Legacy methods for faculty are used at the Royal Melbourne Institute of Technology, now RMIT University, where each online course design contributes to a collection of model courses which faculty study before designing their own courses for peer review for approval before publication. Peer review enables course teams to get explicit feedback—"from comments about the pros and cons of particular strategies to specific editorial and technical suggestions"—and reviewers see how the work others do may apply to their own teaching. In reviewing courses, faculty typically recommend improvements for areas that the course creators may have overlooked:

- A lack of clarity in linking resources and activities to learning outcomes;
- A lack of flexibility in catering for diverse groups of students;
- Failure to link to strategic priorities (i.e., internationalization or work-integrated learning);
- Failure to link to activities in addition to resources;
- Inclusion of extraneous buttons; and
- Unclear navigation strategies.

RMIT wants to emphasize its core values: courses are expected to show evidence of design, of peer review, and of "forward thinking through an evaluation plan" that enables continuous improvement "because we want our students to experience a unified program rather than a variety of isolated classes. Moreover, we are interested in seeing how our online courses contribute to the total learning experience each student has" [45].

In this information age, we are perhaps more aware of time as a sacred commodity. In designing courses that build community and create legacies and set high expectations for each student and for themselves, online teachers should know that interaction takes time, as Michael Moore notes:

> I should add here that, in my own online teaching, I have been reminded yet again, as I have discovered over a lifetime of involvement in distance education, that the distant learner, adult and highly competent in life though he/she may be, does have a much greater need for the

> instructor's emotional support, for reassurance that everything is "going okay," than most educators in the classroom will find believable. It is a phenomenon not to be underestimated as one attends to the need to balance the cost of "time and effort" with the desire to provide a quality experience [46].

Early in the online course, perhaps even more so than in the traditional classroom, explain Coppola, Hiltz, and Rotter, it is critically important to establish "swift trust"—the willingness to suspend doubt about whether others who are "strangers" can be counted on to work on the group's task—by building in early activities that set positive expectations, successful learning and high levels of responsiveness [47]. Designing for constructive, agentive, collaborative learning, Islam advocates building androgogical curricula that allow choice and self-direction, that are practical and problem centered, that capitalize on learners' prior knowledge and experiences, and that promote self esteem and respect for individual learners:

> In other words, the old trainer axiom: "tell them what you're going to tell them, tell them, then tell them what you told them" is not androgogy. Androgogy is more like "ask them what they want to know, ask them how and when they would like to learn it, and then ask if you were successful in helping them learn it" [18].

B. Cost Effectiveness: Put First Things First

The goal of the cost effectiveness pillar is to make online learning more accessible by making it more affordable for learners and for providers. From the provider perspective, cost effectiveness is inextricably linked to its commitment to quality and the image or brand it wants to present to the public, to its alumni and supporters, and to its current and prospective constituents. From the faculty perspective, cost effectiveness includes the time and effort involved in designing and teaching (more about this in the discussion of the faculty satisfaction pillar). And from the learner perspective, cost effectiveness may mean shopping for comparative value. From all perspectives, quality implies that value is a function of benefits divided by costs. Ideally, the goal of cost effectiveness is that the price, the cost and the benefits of online programs will be equivalent or better than the price, the costs and the benefits of place-based programs, while still conveying the quality, core values and commitment of the institution. Large-scale implementations that are committed to improving productivity and learning outcomes with approximately the same faculty effort have a better likelihood of producing sustainable programs. In sum, according to Mayadas:

We can assess the degree of institutional commitment by noting answers to four questions:

- Are more than a few faculty involved?
- Is the institution contributing a significant amount of its own resources to the ALN effort?
- Does the institution have a strategic vision for a complete suite of student services; and
- Does the institution have a strategic vision for making ALN a core, financially viable activity? [2]

Institutional commitment to online programs includes the very important step of aligning online delivery with the institution's core values and distinctive mission. From this perspective, cost effectiveness means continually searching for ways to reduce costs, to diminish time and effort, and to increase benefits. To do so, institutions adopt various business models for managing online programs. In an overview of business models, the *Chronicle of Higher Education* article, "Is Anyone Making Money on Distance Education," shows six institutional approaches to measuring costs, and concludes that although costs may be greater than anticipated, so may the benefits [48].

1. Benefits: Teaching, Learning, Discovery, Growth

Many online programs have encountered double-digit annual enrollment increases [49], which serve the goal of achieving capacity enrollment, and at the same time, challenge infrastructure to support rapid growth. Many programs have invested heavily in technology, training, and course development, expecting return on investment to break even in only a few years.

In addition to growth, another significant benefit researchers cite is the effect of online pedagogy on pedagogy institution-wide. At the University of Illinois Graduate School of Library and Information Science (GSLIS), for example, Estabrook cites the benefits of online programs as increasing income potential and job fulfillment for tech-savvy graduates, and shows how training faculty for online teaching has positively affected classroom teaching. The GSLIS program has enabled the department and the faculty to assert leadership, overcome regulatory obstacles, integrate technology into all of their teaching, align their program with emerging trends in the field, increase student retention, gain valuable publicity and research opportunities, and become more entrepreneurial [50]. Similarly, at SUNY Learning Networks, faculty are nine times as likely to report more systematic design of instruction in their online courses; and 85% find that developing and teaching online is a catalyst for improving classroom teaching [51].

Pillar Reference Manual

A perhaps unexpected benefit of online programs is the increased use of continuous assessment for measuring progress—another practice that affects classroom instruction. If, in the past, class evaluations were regarded as "minimally useful," says Harden, "that may be the result of the fact that the former technologies being used—podiums, chalk, and chalkboards—didn't need to be assessed. Institutions weren't spending $500,000 to roll out that kind of technology platform. Today, the technology rollouts are much more complex and expensive, so it's critical that schools have an evaluation system . . . . Capturing system-wide information on a learning process is a lot harder than it looks" [52].

Yet collaborative help for cost effective practices is readily available. Because schools share similar challenges and because the Internet enables greater communication, faculty and administrators are sharing cost-effective teaching practices and techniques in-house and in public forums such as the World Lecture Hall, Merlot, the TLT group, the Centre for Curriculum, Transfer, and Technology, the American Distance Education Consortium, Educause, the Knowledge Media Lab and more [53, 54,55, 56, 57, 58, 59]. In an essay for the Educational Pathways Newsletter, Jeffrey Feldberg lists tips for effective, inexpensive course development that include using course designers who can arrange content in an HTML editor more quickly than most faculty can; addressing learning styles with text, graphics and audio; and using independent reviewers of course efficacy [60]. Steve Gilbert describes ways to use "low threshold applications" (LTAs), low cost technology for teaching in ways that are easy to learn, inexpensive, "already almost ubiquitous," not intimidating, and with observable positive consequences [61].

Innovative partnerships conserve resources by sharing them. Academic libraries are restructuring to "unlock the potential of their intellectual property" [62], sharing resources for searches at the Collaborative Digital Reference Service [63]. The Internet Public Library makes more than 19,000 full texts available online [64], and academic libraries and publishers at 12 universities are working to create a joint e-publishing venture that may be linked to the online catalog the Lincoln Library group already operates [65]. In April 2002, the Massachusetts Institute of Technology announced its intention to make the materials from its courses freely available for noncommercial use [66]. Online learning brings new, more public attention to the quality of pedagogy and higher learning while it opens doors far wider than the one-to-one "ideal" paradigm.

2. New Costs: Infrastructure, Training, Rewards

Projecting costs in a fluctuating, evolving market is complex; the business models that work are characterized by "scalability, interoperability, consistency, and flexibility" [67]. As the University of Maryland University College's (UMUC) Bishop and SchWeber point out, technology is constantly changing and that makes it difficult to project long-term costs. IT employees are much in demand, and schools sometimes lose them to higher-paying competitors. Salaries and incentives for recruiting, training, releasing, and retaining effective instructors may require negotiations throughout an institution's policy making groups. "New cost ingredients such as 'intellectual property' need a conceptual framework for cost analysis because such issues as 'course content ownership' have not been clearly defined or quantified." Considerations like these lead large-scale providers to engage in dialogue and collaboration with other institutions facing the challenges of a competitive marketplace [68]. Yet, if the primary expenses of online programs carry increased costs for start up, for technology and support staff, for faculty incentives, and for communication and server hosting, says Hislop, these costs can be favorably compared with the usually hidden physical plant and capital costs of the university, so that "with all costs included, the two delivery modes are similar in operational cost" [69].

At Penn State, where the World Campus "function[s] as a business within the academic culture," and where each program is expected to become self-reliant within its first few years, a rigorous system of CQI has been implemented to achieve specific, controlled growth projections by evaluating all operations in terms of the scope of the market, in terms of streamlining and synergizing procedures, and in terms of scalability [70]. Wherever possible, World Campus wants to integrate online operations with its traditional operations to present its image of excellence to the public. World Campus shares its successful project to redesign its website to present a consistent, learner-centered image of the World Campus at the Sloan-C™ site designed for people to benefit by sharing their insights about what works best in online learning [31].

3. Methods and Resources: Re-thinking and Shifting

"A fundamental shift in thinking" is needed to make use of cost efficiencies: "Rather than focus on how to provide more effective and efficient teaching, colleges and universities must focus on how to produce more effective and efficient student learning." To do so, schools need "a comprehensive planning methodology" and "examples of practice that prove the theory" [71]. Bearing in mind that the costs of online learning "are highly dependent upon the kind of telelearning one is talking about" [72], the Pew Monograph on "Improving Learning and Reducing Costs: Redesigning Large Enrollment

Courses" gives examples from four institutions that improved learning, efficiency, and costs by capitalizing on design features that enable more students to enroll in high-demand courses *without adding to faculty workload*. "Once it is possible for institutions to create a surplus of instructional resources rather than simply consuming them, we will be forced to rethink many of our assumptions about planning and budgeting" [73].

To maintain consistent quality that reflects its mission in-class and online, the University of Maryland University Campus (UMUC) uses a model that links quality and cost. UMUC asks two basic questions about costs: "'Which quality alternatives will produce a specified level of effectiveness for least cost?' And 'Which quality alternatives will produce the highest level of effectiveness for a fixed amount?'" Linking cost to quality, UMUC budget decisions focus on four key indicators:

- Student support
- Faculty support
- Curriculum development and delivery
- Evaluation and assessment

UMUC evaluates each initiative in terms of the relation of cost to impact, so that UMUC can maintain and improve quality. Of critical importance is the insight that institutions are unique, and so each institution "must develop models that fit the organizational culture, commitment, and resources" [74]. For example, we would expect that institutions that focus on populations defined by prior success, gender, ethnicity, region, religion or culture would use radically different indices for quality according to their unique missions. As pillar editor for Sloan-C™ effective practices in cost effectiveness, Tana Bishop emphasizes that identifying the institution's primary quality indicators is the first step for determining cost effectiveness [31].

Several studies are especially useful resources for measuring and comparing costs. The Pew Learning and Technology Program makes available a course-planning tool, accompanied by examples [75]. The Centre for Curriculum, Transfer, and Technology has developed an online, interactive check sheet useful for choosing or designing a course management system (CMS) [76]; and Brian Morgan of Marshall University provides an interactive worksheet to estimate costs and return on investment [77]. Dennis Jones of the National Center for Higher Education Management Systems created a Technology Costing Methodology that is proposed as a tool to analyze costs using a standard methodology; version 1.0, updated January 9, 2002 is available online [78]. The American Council of Education Center for Policy Analysis provides a wealth of resources to support its national awards for Academic Excellence and Cost Management [79], as does the Mellon Foundation Initiative on Cost Effective Uses of Technology in Teaching [80]. In

II. The Pillars

February 2002, the National Association of College and University Business Officers (NACUBO) released its uniform methodology for identifying the costs of delivering undergraduate education; the one-page reporting form is a helpful overview of direct and indirect costs [81]. And, in "The Costs and Costing of Networked Learning," Greville Rumble provides a thought provoking, comprehensive review of current approaches to costing and the current range of cost comparisons—to "stimulate others to undertake more cost studies—if only to ensure that we know the costs of the direction upon which we now seem to be embarked" [82].

Although cost effectiveness profiles of schools vary widely according to mission, pricing and costing structure, endowment, and state and federal regulations governing operations, size, reach, tuition and more, the quality of learning is intrinsically connected to the quality of the choices each institution makes, as William Graves explains:

> Many would argue that the reason for attending a prestigious liberal arts college or private research university as an undergraduate lies more in the delayed value of having gone there than in the education received while there. It is less a case of getting the education you pay for than of paying for what you really want: membership in a lifetime club which offers continuing social and economic advantages to its members. This argument ignores the strictly educational advantages that might reasonably be expected to accrue to a high tuition base, and is not meant to suggest that educational expenditures have no bearing on educational quality. But the trend toward distributed education is in part a response to the escalating cost basis of the traditional higher education enterprise and the possibilities for cost containment enabled by technology. Indeed, if the concept of a quality liberal education based on educational rather than socioeconomic precepts is to survive as a broadly available common-good privilege it must do so on terms that do not equate quality with price but instead seek to contain costs [83].

As institutions seek not only to explain quality costs, but to reduce them [84], while using technology to improve learning and access, the prospect of wider access for a highly educated populace draws closer.

C. Access: Think Win/Win

Wider access is a win for learners, a win for providers, and a win for society. The access pillar means that all qualified, motivated students can complete courses, degrees or programs in the disciplines of their choice. Broadening access to education means that access to courses and to services is available without special equipment beyond a computer with Internet connection.

Certainly, general access to the Internet is growing. In February 2002, the United States Commerce Department announced a 26% gain in Internet usage over the year before: in 2001, 54%, or 143 million of the national population accessed the Internet, averaging a growth of 2 million users per month. The report from National Center for Educational Statistics on "Distance Education at Postsecondary Institutions: 1997-98" found that 79% of public four-year institutions, and 72% of public two-year institutions offered online courses in 1998 to 1.6 million distance learners, projecting that another 20% of institutions planned to start programs by 2001[85]. The annual Campus Computing Report for 2001 indicates that the proportion of "students who own computers is rising, up to almost of three fourths (71.5 percent) of all students in 2001, compared to 58.6 percent in 2000" [86]. Yet a digital divide threatens greater separation between those who have access to information and those who don't [87].

1. Scaffolding: Infrastructure and Course Management

"The most obvious factor influencing students' satisfaction with distance learning is convenience of access;" however, access blocked by technical difficulty is the most frequent complaint, observe Thompson and McGrath [88].

Obviously, creating reliable, affordable access is essential for effective learning. User-friendly access requires complex decisions about choosing, funding, implementing, and maintaining adequate infrastructure, including course management systems [89]. Some features of network-enabled, interactive access that include email, FTP, peer-to-peer cooperative learning and teamwork, archived knowledge, performance reports, accessing and searching materials, animation, tutorials, bulletin boards, discussions, demonstrations, and immediate feedback and performance reporting—these features can enhance learning, satisfaction, cost effectiveness and scalability [90]. But while prices from the leading course management system vendors range from courseware at $5000 per server to $2,000,000 for end-to-end support for large institutional systems, "CMS Users Are Still Waiting for the Killer App" according to an Eduventures report, which lists the major factors in CMS decisions as: ease of use (64%), flexibility (47%) and price (46%). To design the features they want most—ease of use, flexibility, and

II. The Pillars

price—"a sizable percentage of institutions still [use] homegrown systems" rather than license from commercial vendors [91]. At eArmyU where many schools offer programs using many platforms, the PricewaterhouseCoopers' portal wants to enable learners to get access to any component of its services within 3 clicks of a mouse. Of particular interest may be this list of desirable access features for CMSs that eArmyU developed during its first year of experience with 24 schools. The list includes features that promote facility and interaction. You will notice in the list below that usage and progress metrics are built into eArmyU's design specifications for CMSs that enable faculty, learners and administrators to measure usage and progress.

Table 2: eArmyU's Design Specifications for CMSs
(excerpted from eArmyU's RFP for prospective partners
http://www.earmyu.com/public/public_about-auao_become-a-partner.asp)

Courses
Courses are capable of being launched and operated within an HTML frameset.
Course content is organized with the following categories or equivalent: Course Administration (for Instructors only), Announcements, Staff Information, Course Information, Calendar, Communication, Assignments, Course Documents, External Links, Course Map, Course Homepage, Assessment Tools, Student Tools, and Course Usage.
Course is configured to allow first page of course to be displayed immediately after successfully authenticating with host institution CMS.
Course displays campus branding (e.g., wordmark, logo, typography, and color scheme) on every page.
Course Administration
Instructor(s) can create new course offering using a course creation wizard.
Instructor(s) can customize course settings and presentation (images, etc.).
Instructor(s) can easily access tools to create, edit, and manage courses from one location.
Announcements
Instructor(s) can post upcoming class events and other announcements.
Students can view upcoming class events and other announcements.
Class events and other announcements can be sorted and viewed in the following ways: "Today," "Last 7 Days," "Last 30 Days," and "All Announcements."
Staff Information
Instructor(s) can create and edit current contact information for the course.
Students can view up-to-date contact information for the course.

Pillar Reference Manual

Course Information
Instructor(s) can create and edit course information for the course.
Students can view course information for the course.

Calendar
Instructor(s) can create and edit important deadlines related to the course.
Students can view important deadlines related to the course.
Calendar information can be viewed by Day, by Week, by Month, and by Course.
Calendar information is presented by categories (e.g.. Assignments, Appointments, Reminders, and Events).

Communication
Instructor(s) can create a forum for questions and answers.
Instructor(s) can create and view sort-able discussion archives.
Students/Instructor(s) can participate in a forum with questions and answers.
Instructor(s) and students can share questions and answers related to the course using discussion forums. Users can share text messages as well as bitmap and vector based art, with tools to create text and other messages.
Searchable forums (e.g., by keyword, by author) with ability to display multiple forum discussion threads.
Synchronous chat rooms for individuals and groups.
Students can create private discussion areas, restricting access from other students (viewable by Instructor(s)).
Instructor(s) and students can share questions and answers related to the course using email addresses available within the course.
Instructor(s) and students can share questions and answers related to the course by visiting group homepages.
Instructor(s) and students can share contact information with one another by accessing a student roster.

Assignments
Instructor(s) can create and update assignments.
Assignments can be created to be reviewed or audited and graded.
Students can submit assignments for review and grading purposes.

II. The Pillars

Course Documents
All the course content for each class is centrally located within the Course Management System.
Instructor(s) can add documents to the course of any file format and provide descriptive text for the document.
Students can view / download course documents.
External Links
Instructor(s) can add and edit links to external websites to supplement course materials.
Instructor(s) can track student usage of these links.
Students can view and follow links to external websites.
Course Map/Course Contents
Centrally located, comprehensive list of course content on one page.
Course Homepage
Students can create a personal web page for the course.
Assessment Tools
Instructor(s) can view ad hoc statistical reports of completed quizzes and surveys.
Quizzes and surveys can be randomized.
Student Tools
Instructor(s) can create robust quizzes and surveys with guided creation wizards.
Instructor(s) can view ad hoc statistical reports of completed quizzes and surveys.
Students can complete quizzes and surveys online.
Notification of completion occurs immediately after completing the quiz or survey with a confirmation screen. The screen provides basic information about the quiz or survey (e.g., Course Title, Course Instructor, Survey Name).
Notification of completion is sent to student via email immediately after completion if the survey or quiz. The email contains basic course information as well as Grade and Percentile information.

Pillar Reference Manual

Course Usage
Instructor(s) can view information about course usage and in multiple formats (e.g., Summary, by Section, by Student).
Course usage statistics are generated ad hoc and displayed in graphics and charts [92].

CMSs affect learning, teaching, affordability, and satisfaction. Many educators seriously object to the rigid requirements of uniform platforms that do not easily adapt to creative, active and constructive learning designs [93]. Thus, consultant Michael Feldstein emphasizes that we are overdue for course management systems with greater educational potential:

> Systems [purchasers] will continue to be disappointed with overpriced, over-hyped, poorly implemented, and poorly documented software that supplies none of the promised benefits. The SCORM specifications will begin to be better understood, although they won't result in substantial breakthroughs in actual products until 2003. Substantial Open Source e-learning platform alternatives will show up on the market for the first time. "Community" will continue to be a hot topic, although failure rates in implementations will remain high. [In 2002] Substantial Open Source e-learning platform alternatives will show up on the market for the first time [94].

2. Learning Support Services

As consumers, learners expect more than reliable connectivity. They expect the kind of service they experience in other service relationships. Enabling learners to get support online rather than requiring them to visit a physical location enhances accessibility and satisfaction. Geith and Vignare observe that online students are sophisticated shoppers who evaluate their potential relationships with institutions from a service perspective.

Granger and Benke agree that "successful student support is a result of every aspect of a program, from a prospective student's first awareness of the program to graduation day, working in an integrated fashion to maintain the student's engagement and progress. Students find programs supportive not because there is a Coordinator of Student Support available from 9 to 3 to solve their problems, but because the program was designed with the student perspective in mind" [95]. Who knows better than the learner what the

II. The Pillars

obstacles are? Clearly, satisfactory learning experiences lead to more learning and extend to lifelong learning. Thus, a steady stream of feedback from learners can enable teachers and administrators to implement improvements rapidly [96].

At Penn State's World Campus, McGrath and colleagues advise: "Effective online programs must 'unlearn' traditional ideas of supporting students and, instead, determine which support services to offer distance students based on feedback from the students themselves." The World Campus online environment includes administrative, instructional, advising, counseling, and activities and services that promote a sense of community and strong, ongoing relationships. Penn State's World Campus creates a sense of community and connection to the university through many avenues: audio conferences, discussion groups, bulletin boards, program offices, online chats, Penn State logos, web site links, extra curricular resources, a peer mentor program, and a student advisory board. To these services is added an important ethical dimension: advisors assure that the World Campus and particular program are right for the student based on the student's background and educational and career goals [97]. In 1999, Thompson provided a preview of World Campus's plan for online services that have now been implemented and expanded [98]. World Campus has also added a 24x7 toll free help desk.

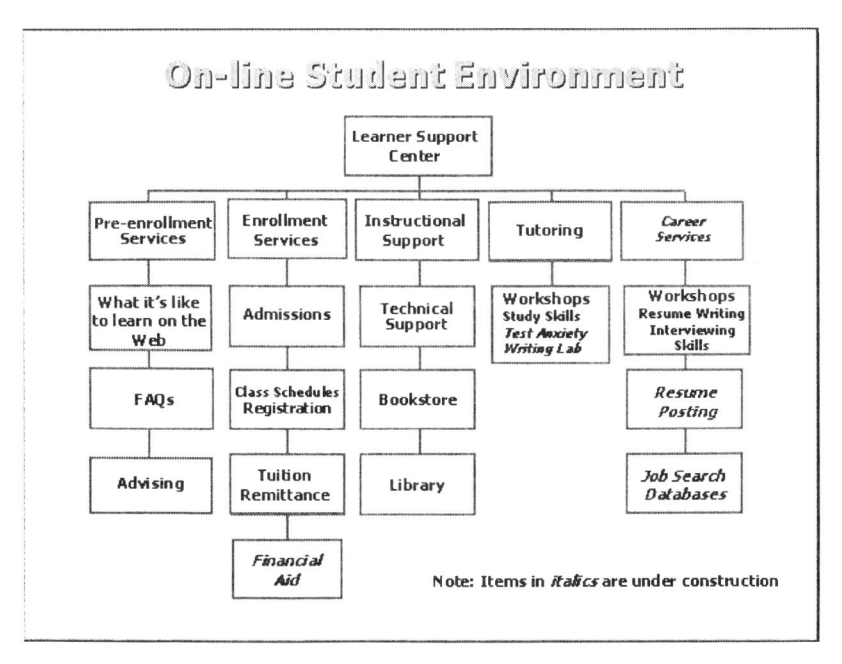

Figure 4: Online Services

On-line Student Environment

- Learner Support Center
  - Pre-enrollment Services
    - What it's like to learn on the Web
    - FAQs
    - Advising
  - Enrollment Services
    - Admissions
    - Class Schedules Registration
    - Tuition Remittance
    - Financial Aid
  - Instructional Support
    - Technical Support
    - Bookstore
    - Library
  - Tutoring
    - Workshops Study Skills *Test Anxiety Writing Lab*
  - Career Services
    - Workshops Resume Writing Interviewing Skills
    - Resume Posting
    - Job Search Databases

Note: Items in *italics* are under construction

Because access to services affects success, and because first impressions may make or break decisions to enroll, the Southern Regional Board and the Ohio State University Environmental Education and Training Partnership provide insightful guidelines for creating more user friendly, more intuitively designed education websites and portals [99, 100].

The Western Cooperative for Educational Telecommunications (WCET) emphasizes that an important component of providing services is describing the specific services available to disabled students. To make all web pages accessible, a text-only version of all Web pages that conform to the World Wide Web Consortium (W3C) Content Accessibility Guidelines is ideal: "These guidelines emphasize the importance of providing text equivalents of non-text content such as images, prerecorded audio, and video" [95]. WCET also recommends Bobby Approval as an easy way to analyze institution's pages [101, 102].

To bring greater national attention to the ways institutions can present truly learner-centered focuses, WCET has produced a guide for effective online student services with examples and a tour of dozens of institutions in online service areas. (Note that WCET's guide was projected to remain current until September 2001 because of rapid changes to the exemplar websites; the guide is followed by a continuing project, "Beyond the Administrative Core: Creating Web-based Student Services for Online Learners.") [103].

Among promising directions, John Sener, Sloan-C™ pillar editor for access, predicts that with decreasing costs and technological advances will come truly effective portals that will deliver a full array of options for students, perhaps providing access to instruction even at the modular level as more schools develop truly learner-centered services and instruction that accommodates, rather than screens, learners [31].

3. The Future of Access: Mind to Mind*

To make learning software "accessible, interoperable, durable, reusable, adaptable and affordable" the Advanced Distributed Learning (ADL) initiative promises to open new partnerships among the federal government, private-sector technology suppliers, and the broader education and training community by using a Shareable Content Object Reference Model (SCORM™) for formulating voluntary guidelines that will enable "the highest quality of education and training tailored to individual needs, delivered cost effectively, anywhere, anytime" [104]. While the SCORM™ model is still developing, ADL's vision of affordable access is gaining

---

*At the Sloan Summer Workshop in 2001, Burks Oakley suggested that the ideal access is "mind to mind."

support and interest—its December 2001 conference included 30 Learning Management Systems vendors, 23 authoring tool vendors, 50 learning content providers, and 380 participants in the technical testbed event. Also in December 2001, the Southern Regional Board—a consortium of colleges and universities in Alabama, Arkansas, Delaware, Florida, Georgia, Kentucky, Louisiana, Maryland, Mississippi, North Carolina, Oklahoma, South Carolina, Tennessee, Texas, Virginia, and West Virginia focusing on ways to remove barriers to higher education—joined the ADL initiative [105]. The Massachusetts Open Knowledge Initiative (OKI) and The IMS Global Learning Consortium have also joined with ADL to seek ways to open learning and administrative systems for greater interoperability within and among institutions [106,107].

As access widens in ways we have yet to discover, Randy J. Hinrichs, Group Research Manager of Microsoft's Learning Sciences and Technology, expects that:

> We're going to see significant new thinking in e-learning with a programmable web freeing innovation. Some changes: partnerships among government agencies, software industries, and universities will focus on technologies that enhance activity-based learning, embedded assessment, immersive collaboration, and extended mobile computing with less importance placed on lecturing and test-taking. You'll see new highly collaborative and visual technologies for education such as gaming and simulations. Quality assurance will be the cornerstone for proof of investment and assessment validation. The accreditation boards will take a harder look at how to accredit these environments as they emerge, especially in science, technology, engineering, and math. And most important, learning will start being fun, and, in some cases, enchanting [94].

D. Faculty Satisfaction: Seek First to Understand

The faculty satisfaction pillar means that faculty experience online teaching as effective and professionally beneficial. The availability of qualified and enthusiastic faculty enables institutions to respond to growing demands for online learning and to maintain and improve the quality of learning effectiveness. Newman and Scurry imply that faculty skill online brings greater attention than traditional classroom skill:

Institutions skilled in the use of technology to improve learning will soon be seen as more dynamic and effective than their less engaged competitors. Therefore, institutions and faculty members viewing themselves as excellent at teaching now must excel in the use of technology as well, if they are to remain leaders. How should the institution support faculty members as they make that transition? [108]

The demand for faculty, and particularly for online teachers, is expected to grow 36% or more in the next ten years with an expected increase in population of 18-24 year olds and a growing demand for lifelong learning [109]. At the same time, there is a steadily increasing use of adjuncts [110]. With numbers like these, it makes sense for everyone to understand more about what satisfies faculty. Interestingly, the National Center for Education Statistics report on distance learning in 1998, including online learning, reveals little difference in satisfaction levels among distance education teachers and their peers who teach on campus, despite a higher workload for online faculty [111]. What do faculty find especially satisfying about teaching online?

1. Faculty Benefits: Diversity, Reach, Interdisciplinarity

For faculty, the benefits of teaching online are the benefits of teaching face-to-face: enjoying and being able to communicate and relate well with students, motivating learning, and using self-motivated inquiry and analysis to pursue and disseminate knowledge. "The principal reward . . . is the opportunity to extend the reach of your teaching to students who otherwise would not be able to learn from you. As these students may be from anywhere in the world, incorporating them into your classes can result in a geographical and cultural blend from which each participant, including the instructor, can learn" [112]. Although it is to be expected that learning and satisfaction levels among faculty will differ according to the institution's commitment to its online programs in terms of integrating online programs with overall institutional objectives, some common themes emerge from metrics used to survey faculty.

According to the University of Central Florida's study of nearly 180 faculty from its five colleges, "institutionalizing faculty development for ALN delivery has proven beneficial" because it:

- Provides experiential learning for faculty participants
- Fosters cross-discipline sharing of teaching techniques
- Builds learning communities among faculty

- Creates lifelong learners among faculty
- Creates discussion of the teaching and learning process
- Allows peer evaluation of successes and failures
- Exposes faculty to tools and instructional best practices
- Models a combination of delivery techniques
- Uses cooperative and collaborative learning techniques
- Provides greater flexibility for busy faculty
- Transforms all teaching for more active student-centered learning [11]

In Volume 1 of *Online Education* and in a special issue of the *Journal of Asynchronous Learning Networks*, studies of faculty satisfaction at the University of California, University of Illinois, Penn State's World Campus, and the State University of New York Learning Network confirm the University of Central Florida's summary of the benefits of online teaching and elaborate on each of the benefits from a variety of faculty perspectives. In addition to the benefits listed above, faculty and teaching assistants involved in scaling up ALNs for large courses at the University of Illinois [113,114], at Michigan State University [19], at Vanderbilt University [115], at the University of Florida [116], and at Brigham Young University [117] are pleased with initiatives that automate some feedback and alleviate the burden of routine activities such as quizzing, reminding, acknowledging receipt, some grading, randomizing problem-solution assignments, and answering frequent non-course related questions. Faculty at the University of Illinois benefit from interdisciplinary insights they gain from ALN programs for Writing Across the Curriculum in composition and pedagogy, electrical engineering, computing, and writing technologies [118].

In a SUNY study involving 255 instructors from 31 colleges, faculty report being happy about the positive effects of online teaching on classroom teaching, and especially about quantity and quality of interaction online among learners and with instructors, which faculty compare favorably with interaction in the classroom. Finding that 91% of faculty believe the online environment is appropriate for teaching a wide variety of courses, the SUNY study illustrates that faculty appreciate the mentoring function of teaching online:

> It's very clear to me that the students are the real teachers in online courses—mini lectures; and all the other devices are simply resources that they can call upon. I find it somewhat amusing to read how some entrepreneurs believe that the Internet offers them the "advantage" of hiring and using virtuoso teachers. In my opinion these "star" performers are relegated to entertainers on the web.

> I say again: The real teaching is done through peer discussion with the formal instructor adopting the role of moderator [51].

In the SUNY study, faculty believe they spend more time on teaching and reflecting about teaching and less time rushing and worrying about discipline and non-academic matters. Important elements of online faculty satisfaction include learning with a greater diversity of students, and gaining greater opportunities for leadership, research, publication, recognition, collegiality, and professional development. Depending on the climate of institutional support, faculty satisfaction metrics demonstrate strong endorsement. In the SUNY system, at Herkimer County Community College, the results of the fourth year of a faculty satisfaction study include these benchmarks:

- 97% of faculty observe greater student to student interaction in online classes
- 96% of faculty believe the quality of interaction online is higher
- 84% of faculty observe greater student to professor interaction in online classes
- 91% of faculty believe the quality of student to professor interaction is higher
- 100% of faculty intend to continue teaching online
- 82% of faculty see a positive impact on classroom teaching because of teaching online
- 100% of faculty are satisfied with online teaching
- 100% of faculty intend to continue teaching online [51]

2. Faculty Resistance: Time, Authority, Recognition

Nevertheless, resistance to teaching online remains strong. The Campus Computing Project report estimates that while 80% of colleges and universities make tools available to faculty, only 20.6% of college courses use web-based course management tools. Diane Lynch observes that faculty have reason to resist:

> Technology presents the kinds of pressures that many of us would rather just ignore—a strategy that has worked pretty well so far. Technology raises all kinds of troublesome issues, most obviously the plain and annoying fact that it takes a lot of time and effort to figure out how to use it. It's a professional pain in the neck in a hundred different ways—and, at least according to the most recent study that the Higher Education Research Institute at the

II. The Pillars

> University of California at Los Angeles has conducted on the topic, it's a source of stress for the majority of us. So how do we cope? In every other segment of the economy, technology has triggered rethinking, reshaping, and, yes, even downsizing. Not so in the academy. Faced with marketplace pressures and private-sector competition, many of us cry academic freedom and a higher calling, and we proceed with business as usual. The good news for faculty members is that administrators can't really force us to change. They can cajole, they can dangle grant money in front of our faces, they can pay the tab to send us to syllabus conferences. But when it comes to putting our courses on the Web, or using new software programs as part of our instruction, or participating in chat rooms with our students, we can cry academic freedom and simply refuse. We have tenure, and we don't have to if we don't want to [119].

It is worthwhile to seek a better understanding of the reasons faculty have for resisting online teaching because resistance is a quality indicator that merits close attention. Faculty and others who object to online learning may be overworked, underpaid, and under appreciated. Faculty may believe that online learning deprives teachers and learners of interaction and socialization and alienates people, undermines academic freedom, costs more in time and money, relies on yet more under-appreciated adjuncts, lures students away from enrolling in face-to-face classes, threatens intellectual honesty, integrity, and property rights—while offering comparatively little incentive, recognition, and reward. Moreover, tradition values the classroom as a sacred space:

> The faculty identity as a professor, as an expert, as a source of knowledge and information, is heavily shaped and reinforced through the role of classroom instructor and the face-to-face interactions that make up the classroom teaching arrangements. The students in the classroom represent a mirror that shapes the "looking-glass self" and the professorial identity. ALNs entail a different process of identity enhancement. Even if one is willing to entertain an alternative to the teacher-centered classroom model, the computer screen may be viewed as a totally unacceptable alternative for those who shape their identity through face-to-face interaction, an animated teaching performance, and an embodied human response. Asynchronous online computer interaction provides a very

different mirror and set of responses to our presentation of self [120].

Among programs that are conscientiously working to address faculty concerns like the above to make known the value of the online classroom, faculty cite disincentives including increased workloads, institutional reward systems that undervalue web-based activities [121], and unfamiliarity with shared decision making with groups or teams involved in course construction and delivery [122].

Rockwell and colleagues summarize the findings of a study of 237 faculty and administrators that compare endorsement and resistance:

> The primary incentives centered on intrinsic or personal rewards. These rewards included opportunities to provide innovative instruction and apply new teaching techniques as well as self-gratification, fulfilling a personal desire to teach, recognition of their work, and peer recognition. Other incentives included extending educational opportunities beyond the traditional institutional walls so place-bound students have access and release time for faculty preparation. The major perceived obstacles related to time requirements, developing effective technology skills, and assistance and support needs. Monetary awards for faculty and the cost to the student were seen as neither incentives nor obstacles. Faculty were divided on how they saw distance teaching affecting their yearly evaluation process and their promotion/tenure needs; about 40% saw it as an incentive, while about 30% saw it as an obstacle [123].

Kenneth Green, the Director of the Campus Computing Project notes: "The sad irony is that barely one campus in five has expanded the criteria used in the faculty review and promotion process to include technology in research, teaching and scholarship . . . . The institutional message continues to be 'go there—into technology—at your own risk'" [124]. Because "many senior and junior faculty expressed great anxiety about the current ambiguity and confusion" about the status of their online work in tenure decisions, the American Association for History and Computing, in conjunction with members of the Modern Language Association and the American Political Science Association, offers guidelines for faculty review [125].

3. Challenges: Wise Design

We teach online in a variety of arrangements. In some programs, online teaching is an expected part of the faculty workload; in some, online teaching is wholly voluntary; and in some, like the University of Phoenix for example, teaching faculty are mostly adjuncts whose work is evaluated by full time faculty members. In each of these arrangements, one common practice is a hallmark of quality in online learning: thoughtful training. It is centrally important when online teachers become online learners and, by the same token, when online learners become online teachers—that metrics guide continuous improvement.

In "Net-Learning: Strategies for On-Campus and Off-Campus Network-enabled Learning," Bourne provides models for online programs according to the likelihood of their adoption by various kinds of institutions. For each kind of institution, Bourne points to reductions in cost and time: Once materials are developed, new instructors can be acclimated much more quickly; when customization is easy, and when instructions are complete and replete with exemplars, learners and teams can individualize learning in coherent course structures; and faculty have more time for interaction with learners. Bourne forecasts a shift in faculty time allocation [126]:

Figure 5: Analysis of Time Shifts in Faculty Activities

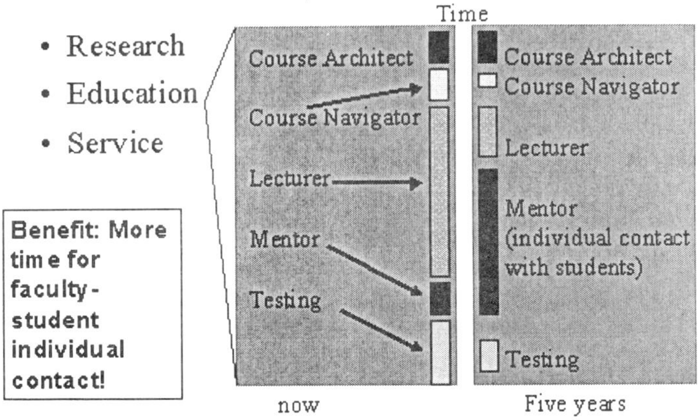
Time
• Research
• Education
• Service
Benefit: More time for faculty-student individual contact!
Course Architect
Course Navigator
Lecturer
Mentor
Testing
now
Course Architect
Course Navigator
Lecturer
Mentor (individual contact with students)
Testing
Five years

At SUNY Learning Networks where online learning includes "1,000 online instructors from fifty-three different colleges offering over 1,500 online courses to more than 25,000 enrollees across the State University of New York," a study indicates that faculty typically devote more than 120 hours to course development with extensive help available to them from SLN.

> We suspected that this level of effort might offer opportunities for reflection that would have a positive impact on classroom-based instruction . . . . It should be pointed out that this development time is not spent alone. All faculties who participate in the SUNY Learning Network agree to participate in rigorous preparatory training, and receive ongoing support during the entire time they teach their courses, both from the trainers, multimedia instructional designers, and a faculty HelpDesk. Training begins with participation in an online all-faculty conference that mirrors the environment in which faculty will eventually instruct. Through participation in this online conference new faculty come together to experience firsthand what they and their students will do in this new learning environment. The all-faculty conference uses the same technology and interface that the new instructors will use, and provides opportunities to discuss a variety of common concerns, observe live courses, and "try out" many of the features and functions they will use in their own online courses, all from the perspective of the student [51].

At the University of Phoenix, faculty effectiveness is continuously developed through several programs: the selection of new faculty and basic training; training for the first online course; mentoring for the first online course; and workshops on writing, critical thinking across the curriculum, grading, evaluation and feedback, learning teams, copyright infringement, dealing with difficult students, web page development for enhancing course presentation, and syllabus preparation [20].

Online faculty are forming virtual networks to enhance collegiality. Faculty of the University of Maryland University Campus Center for Intellectual Property advise colleagues and institutions about online academic honesty and intellectual property [127]. Maryland Online provides training for faculty and showcases their online courses [128]. At Penn State's World Campus, where a goal is to fully integrate online and face-to-face communities, an array of collegial services, news, and resources welcome faculty with recognition, awards, professional development, and opportunities to confer online and in person. At the University of Illinois, Ray Schroeder serves the academic community by helping to inform faculty with daily links to relevant information, posting news about technology and education [129]. Faculty at Indiana University's Center for Research on Learning and Technology compare four online courses with detailed praise for effective strategies and recommendations for improving active learning, feedback, and design [130]. Many programs offer prospective and continuing faculty an array of online training, degree programs and certificates, and resources for teaching excellence.

Yet, despite abundant evidence of faculty enthusiasm for teaching online, and of increasing opportunities for research, professional development, and wider collegiality, many faculty are not always certain that pedagogy rather than technological or commercial interest spurs the growth of online learning [131]. In response, organizations like the National Education Association, the American Federation of Teachers, the Modern Language Association, and the American Association of University Professors insist that faculty must govern curricular decisions and that choice of media is most appropriately a faculty responsibility:

> It is imperative, therefore, that colleges and universities now using or planning to use the new technologies of distance education consider the educational functions these new media are intended to perform and the specific problems they raise. Traditional academic principles and procedures will usually apply to these new media, either directly or by extension, but they will not be applicable in all circumstances. When they are not, new principles and procedures will need to be developed so that the new media will effectively serve the institution's basic educational objectives [132].

Some new principles and procedures are suggested in a World Campus study that finds that while faculty are satisfied with the quality of online learning, they can be dissatisfied with the "shared ownership of both the product and the process [of course development] in this collaborative work environment." Faculty can be frustrated by institutional failures to integrate faculty time and effort with traditional academic responsibilities and rewards. In response to these legitimate concerns, Thompson recommends that institutions clearly communicate expectations, distinguish between real and perceived problems, identity the locus of control and change, and continuously work to enhance the faculty experience [122]. "The most significant influence on the evolution of distance education will not be the technical development of more powerful devices," says Dede, "but the professional development of wise designers, educators, and learners" [9].

To make best use of faculty time and expertise, "postmodern technologies call for a restructuring of universities," according to Saba, who suggests that the professor's job of the future will be to manage a team of subject matter specialists, instructional designers, educational technologists, evaluators, and programmers [133]. Berg finds Saba's model reflected in "Early

Patterns of Faculty Compensation for Developing and Teaching Distance Learning Courses," especially in nontraditional programs in which there is an increase in adjuncts [134]. Regardless of the teaching model institutions may adopt, faculty satisfaction is a central quality issue, one that relies on metrics for improvement, says Michael Moore:

> Obviously, an administration that has valid information about these "time-and-effort" variables needed to produce good quality, and uses that information to make good decisions in making contracts, managing and rewarding faculty (or, on the other hand, the administration that makes bad decisions in that regard), will determine, one way or another, the quality of both the student's and the instructor's experience. That, in turn, will determine the long-run success or failure of the program and, perhaps, the institution itself [46].

Faculty have expressed grave reservations that the role of the online teacher, who may become more of a guide than a sage, represents the deprofessionalization of the academy in favor of its commercialization. When institutions see students as customers—and when students see themselves as customers—how will the quality of learning be affected? As the Sloan-C™ pillar editor for effective practices in faculty satisfaction, Melody Thompson calls for greater development of norms and practices:

> To date, much of the information about the faculty experience in online teaching has been anecdotal and situation specific. Some institutions are implementing cross-institutional and/or cross-discipline studies of the faculty experience to identify commonalities, establish guidelines for practice, and provide the basis for informed planning and decision making [31].

E. Student Satisfaction: Synergize

As the legacy cycle in Figure 1 indicates, continuous quality improvement synergizes thinking and doing, creating and consuming, expert and novice. In a CQI synergy that regards customers as the arbiters of quality, the boundaries between learners and teachers are porous. Effective teachers have always known they learn from students how to teach [135].

The student satisfaction pillar measures students' overall satisfaction with learning, teaching, affordability, and access, and a multitude of metrics seek to define student satisfaction. The National Survey of Student Engagement,

II. The Pillars

for example, measures the quality of learners' experience according to five benchmarks: academic challenge, active and collaborative learning, interactions with faculty, enriching educational experiences, and a supportive environment [42]. Likewise, findings from 3000 student satisfaction responses in 154 Capella University courses confirm important assumptions about student satisfaction with learning online; Rossman lists practices that make online learning more satisfactory for teachers and learners [136].

1. What Learners Want

Generally speaking, learners want to believe in their own ability to learn. In online learning, students expect convenience and evidence that providers have intuited how learners can most effectively achieve their learning goals. At Stanford's Center for Professional Development, Executive Director Anthony DiPaolo lists 20 criteria students desire in online learning:

- Access to learning independent of time and distance
- Convenience and flexibility with a range of course and program delivery options and multiple avenues for learning
- A choice of synchronous, asynchronous, and blended delivery offerings
- Well-designed, engaging, intellectually challenging and continuously updated courses which connect the transfer of learning to doing
- A wide range of online degree, certification and credentialing options
- Emphasis on interactive, goal-oriented, problem-based learning using real, vivid and familiar examples
- Short modules which can be bundled into an interactive learning experience
- Reliable delivery to any Internet platform with consistent navigation and 24/7 technical support
- Provisions for tele-advising, tele-coaching and tele-mentoring
- Participation in a "connected learning community" by active engagement and collaboration with instructors, tutors, peers and experts
- Access to providers with established brand names representing quality, competency, reputation and a recognized customer base
- To customize the learning activity based on personal experience and assessment of knowledge gaps
- To control the scope, sequence and pacing of learning
- To sample courses and review evaluations before registering
- Worldwide access to information and the training to find it

- To collaborate by working in geographically dispersed learning groups
- Outstanding e-support for student services with a focus on "student as customer"
- Continuous, prompt, and meaningful forms of feedback
- Competitive pricing
- Ongoing educational renewal with commitment from providers to support continuous learning

DiPaolo supports the desire for ongoing educational renewal with a comment from Motorola President Christopher Galvin: "We no longer want to hire engineers with a four year degree. We want our employees with a forty year degree" [137]. These days, many of us are accustomed to the truism that we must be lifelong learners if we want to be technologically savvy people, and the National Center for Education Statistics reports a steady increase in learning activities "from 38 percent of those in the population age 18 and above in 1991 to 48 percent in 1999" [138].

2. Why Do Learners Drop Out?

Traditionally, significant measures of student satisfaction are the rates of completion/retention and persistence, because these rates can be taken as indicators of how well schools accomplish what they set out to do. While no reliably significant national statistics are available for retention in online education, analysts at the National Center for Education Statistics examine a host of completion/retention indicators including placement scores, highschool preparation, family income and education background, rigor of prior training, standardized test scores, gender, ethnicity, age, full-time equivalency enrollment loads, urbanicity, geographic region, subject matter and institutionally determined standards of progress—all of which affect success in postsecondary programs. In its report card, "Measuring Up 2000: The State-by-State Report Card for Higher Education," the National Center for Public Policy and Higher Education found that "Nationwide, only half (52%) of full-time, first-time freshmen at four-year institutions earn a bachelor's degree within five years" [139].

Although online completion rates vary from program to program, it is generally believed that when online completions are lower than face-to-face it may be due to unfamiliar or unreliable technology. It may also be that when schedules become too busy, education can easily be dropped [140]. Dutton finds that while online students are more likely to be older, enrolled on a part-time basis, with greater work and child care commitments, and greater technological skill, they are more likely to complete courses when they are enrolled in a greater number of courses [141]. Schrum and Hong

II. The Pillars

find in a survey of experienced online teachers that significant factors to be considered as predictors of student success include access to tools; technology experience; learning preferences; study habits and skills; goals and purposes lifestyle factors; and personal traits and characteristics [142]. At Herkimer County Community College, where researchers report no significant difference between online and face-to-face completion rates [44], William Pelz believes that making sure students know what to expect in terms of time and commitment is an important predictor of success. In his introduction to online teaching, he includes a discussion of Monroe Community College's video web page that describes the "10 Myths About Online Education," a text and video-based introduction to online learning that dispels some false expectations that learners new to online learning may make [143]. Retention also varies according to institutional setting, and tends to be higher in graduate programs that enroll experienced learners than it is among beginning students for reasons such as "work, family, health, and life change," that have little to do with the quality of the course or the delivery media [144]. In a survey of 760 persisting and non-persisting students enrolled in 52 courses, Tello finds that persistence is positively related to the frequency and methods of instructional interaction [145].

In programs in which retention is high, educators point to practices that diminish dropout risk. Several administrators at a variety of Sloan-C™ schools, contributed to the following Sloan-C™ listserv discussion in June 2000 about the complexity of the retention question:

> Howard Deckelbaum, Director of New York University's Information Technologies Institute, attributes 99.2% retention rate among 600 online non credit students for the spring 2000 semester to NYU's support services. "We micro-manage course development and presentation and monitor the courses constantly. We work very closely with the instructional staff and provide one-on-one advisement for all new faculty and for those faculty that need it on a continuing basis. We use several pedagogical models and help faculty choose one that suits them the most. We contract with a local provider for help desk support. This company works with faculty and students until 11 p.m. 7 days a week."
>
> Jacqueline Moloney of the University of Massachusetts at Lowell, where online retention matches in-class retention, agrees that completion demands a great deal of program management. U Mass Lowell has met the in-class retention benchmark by "investing intensive support services to

faculty, maintaining low faculty/student ratios and by building capacity incrementally." Some students, Moloney says, take online courses "anticipating that they will be 'easier' only to find they are at least equally challenging."

At the University of Illinois-Urbana Champaign, Sandy Levin accounts for a 100% completion rate in a master's degree program by citing the program's continual fine-tuning and flexibility in response to student needs. Burks Oakley II, Associate Vice President at the University of Illinois, observes that program level, selectivity, and expense also affect retention: "I don't think we can compare the retention rates observed in online professional post-baccalaureate degree or certificate programs with the retention rates found in online lower-division courses. By definition, post-baccalaureate students already have shown that they can complete a degree—not so with community college students—these students may not have the same study skills and motivation. Students in an IT degree program paying significant tuition at a private institution are very different than community college students who may be paying $50 per credit hour or less. Certainly there is less tuition lost for a community college student who drops." Yet, says Oakley, "if courses are poorly designed (using email and chat rooms) and if the students lack the discipline to go online regularly (anytime-anyplace learning is notime-noplace learning if the students don't log on) and if the instructor doesn't build a learning community and interact regularly with the students, then an online course might not be very motivating for the students and they might drop out in greater numbers."

Though not all online programs achieve 100% retention, predicting retention is not as simple as it might seem, points out John Sener, former Project Director and Instructional Technologist of the Extended Learning Institute at Northern Virginia Community College: "The retention rates between individual faculty teaching the same course in a given semester, or between the same faculty teaching the same course over different semesters, often show greater variability than the difference between on-campus and online courses. Some of our faculty have lower completion/retention rates because they make their courses more demanding and will not compromise on quality standards. Conversely, courses may have higher retention rates because they're easier, watered-down courses; online courses are not immune to this problem."

Student preparation, placement, discipline, learning style, maturity, age, technical proficiency and prior successful online learning experience—these factor into retention ratios. At Drexel, observes Gregory Hislop, Associate Dean, College of Information Science and Technology, "we have seen that good quality student groups can have very high retention rates." When students take enrollment breaks, it can be due to other professional obligations. Hislop notes some students in Drexel's MSIS program "are taking courses online because they have jobs with a lot of travel or other demands that make it difficult to attend traditional classes. It seems reasonable to guess that this sort of job pressure will translate into lower completion rates."

New courses, new teachers, and new technology—all these may affect completion rates. Olin Campbell, Associate Professor of Instructional Psychology and Technology at Brigham Young University, notes that early course versions may have "bugs, difficulties, and lack of differentiation between needs of different users—all symptomatic of any new innovation." A quality improvement approach in which learners are engaged in identifying the trouble spots ensures that online delivery improves: "We did this with an online workshop, and dramatically improved learner retention. In the process we developed automated intelligent agents that provide a new dimension of learning support without requiring more labor. What started as a means to improve completion rate became also a type of tutor that may lead to better learning than in a large classroom" [146].

3. Immeasurable Benefits

Among the most difficult, if not impossible, measures of student satisfaction are measures of the long-term benefits of learning, including online learning. Some of the more intangible benefits can be measured with follow-up studies of graduates. Two years after completing their programs, 34 graduates of programs in rehabilitation counseling and educational leadership reported on some of the more intangible benefits of student satisfaction. Using an adapted version of Harasim's 1992 "Dimensions of Distance Education" assessment tool, students in two online graduate programs were surveyed on 74 student satisfaction items. "Each item has a two-part response and reflects an interaction between 'how well the program met the student's expectations' and student's perception of 'how important the item was to the quality of the program.' In addition to completing the assessment instrument, each graduate described, in his or her own words, the following relevancy of the degree program in relationship to: themselves as students, their customers/students/clients, their department/organization, and their community." The findings confirm the hopes of educators:

> **Relevancy for self**: Graduates reported more knowledge and skills, more-self-confidence, more relevancy to the field of practice, more skill in the use of computer technology, a broader view and understanding of education, improved skills and knowledge in leadership, more peer contacts, and more self-esteem.
>
> **Relevancy for consumers, students, or clients**: Graduates reported being more knowledgeable and better counselors, with a more holistic approach to services, and more resource knowledge, with greater knowledge in instructional methods, improved knowledge of adult learning, and increased responsibility and skills.
>
> **Relevancy for their Department or Organization**: Graduates identified themselves as more qualified to improve services and credibility, with greater opportunities for promotion and leadership, with increased knowledge and skills including improved decision making and leadership skills, with higher qualifications, and increased knowledge about educational issues and human resource development.
>
> **Relevancy to the Community**: Graduates reported they gave better service to the community, improved dynamic relationships and collaboration, increased knowledge of community resources, and improved programs to serve the community, increased leadership roles and decision making, became educated professionals able to assist the community, strengthened educational skills, and increased involvement in decision making in the community.

II. The Pillars

While most comments in the study strongly praised the online experience, graduates wished they had had more time, fewer feelings of isolation, better access and feedback, and continuing communications with the program. The researchers conclude that: "[Online learning] is not an undertaking that can be packaged and delivered without extensive involvement from the learners, the professors, and a full array of support personnel" [147].

Educators at SUNY Learning Networks are similarly cautionary—"It is helpful for us to understand that concerns about anonymity and isolation are not unfounded. We have discovered that it may be wise to focus more efforts on finding ways to help faculty to get to know their online students and we will continue to work in this area." And SUNY Learning Networks educators are also enthusiastic about student surveys that reflect high levels of satisfaction:

> Are these findings relevant to other institutions? We believe they are useful in a number of ways. Online learning environments are not easy to implement successfully. Effort, coordination, planning and expense is required. If an institution is considering systematic implementation of online education it is useful to know that success, as measured by traditional notions of best practice in higher education, is possible.
>
> In general, although we acknowledge that these results may not be completely generalizable to other systems, to know that nearly 1000 students from 53 institutions from associate level through graduate level programs reported high levels of learning and satisfaction in online courses, offered through a single, unified system, is potentially helpful. We feel the success of SLN demonstrates that it is possible to overcome the complexity and challenges involved in system-wide online learning initiatives, to provide increased flexible access, and to maintain high standards across courses [17].

Knowing what to expect during and after online education surely helps learners make informed decisions. But before learners enter a program, how can they determine its value? The larger question about the quality of online learning is addressed in the Pew Monograph "Quality Assurance for Whom?"

Interactive multimedia and other technologies will change how we think about providers and whom we regard as providers. Learning resources that were once only available through education institutions will appear in retail stores in the form of multimedia software and other computer-based courseware. Consumers will be able to purchase learning products independently and learn at their convenience, collectively spending millions of dollars on education each year. This purchasing power will have a tremendous impact on who controls learning [148].

The search for improving learning, affordability, and access, for the time when anyone can learn any time anywhere as an ordinary part of everyday life is the legacy of higher education. Today, the legacy's impact is both personal and public:

> In the age of knowledge, it has become increasingly clear that not only has knowledge become the wealth of nations, it has also become the key to one's personal standard of living, the quality of one's life. Hence, we might well make the case that today it has become the responsibility of democratic societies to provide their citizens with the education and training they need throughout their lives, whenever, wherever, and however they desire it, at high quality, and at a cost they can afford [149].

By what objective measures can learners evaluate learning options? Now that choice no longer depends so much on geography, institutions will need to demonstrate their distinctive value in ways that are more meaningful for people who have more choices:

> The larger task before us is not only to move from capacity and process standards that address physical space to capacity and process standards that address cyberspace; it is to develop standards that address consequences—outcomes, results, competencies—in physical space or cyberspace.
>
> Taking this next step will involve establishing evidence profiles for the success of institutional efforts; developing competency-based accreditation reviews; and creating outcome measures of student achievement. These tasks call for the development of institutional performance indicators that describe desired results in the areas of student learning, research, and service. An increased emphasis on competencies will require paying more attention to what students learn than how they learn it [150].

II. The Pillars

The influential Boyer Commission's 1998 report recommended ways for institutions to pay more attention to improving learning, including focusing on research-based, inquiry-based, and interdisciplinary learning from the beginning of the college experience; linking communication skills and coursework; using information technology creatively; engaging students as apprentice teachers; changing faculty reward systems; and cultivating community. In its 2002 follow-up report, the Boyer Commission calls for more comprehensive progress:

> Although there are many good practices in place, they tend to be scattered and/or offered on a small scale. The first step is for universities to expand, integrate, and sustain current good practices so that they are central to the undergraduate experience [151].

The purpose of the quality framework is exactly this: to expand, integrate, and sustain effective practices in each of the five pillars. Institutions can use the framework to identify and profile core academic values that demonstrate their institutional excellences with empirical evidence. How close are we to realizing the vision of quality education accessible to all? As practitioners of online education have shown, the elements of effective learning, affordability, access, and faculty and student satisfaction positively affect all of us in a continuously evolving legacy.

Pillar Reference Manual

III. The Quality Framework: Sharpen the Saw

Sharpening the saw is a metaphor for using tools to get better results. There is always room for improvement, and to get the results we want we have to be able to envision the shapes of success. The quality framework, a tool for continuously improving online programs in higher education, provides ways of demonstrating distinctive institutional quality. As institutions continuously improve pedagogy, and as technology evolves, the framework itself is a work in progress, designed to facilitate the sharing of effective practices among institutions. You will notice, as you consider your own perspectives on access, that this version of the framework is a quality floor, based on general guidelines rather than on the unique practices and metrics of quality which discrete institutions might choose to add or modify. Readers are invited to comment on the framework and to share effective practices at: http://www.sloan-c.org/effectivepractices.

The five pillars, learning effectiveness, access, student satisfaction, faculty satisfaction, and cost effectiveness, support the quality framework. For each of the pillars, the framework enables institutions to set the goals, to identify supporting practices and resources, and to project and measure timely progress towards the goals. As illustrated in Figure 6, below, the pillars are interdependent so that what institutions do in each area affects outcomes in all areas.

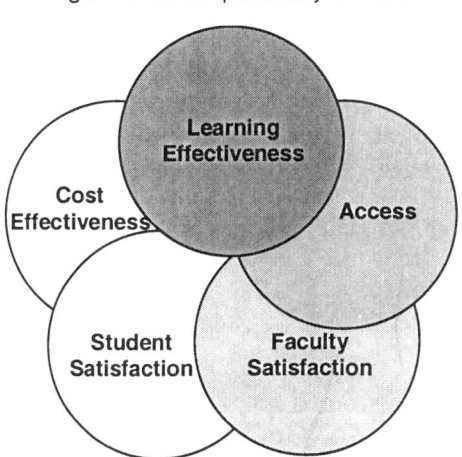

Figure 6: Interdependency of Pillars

Pillar Reference Manual

The pillars of the quality framework are flexible enough to include alternatives as understood and applied by each institution as appropriate to its distinctive quality. Here is an overview of the basic principles of pillars of the quality framework:

LEARNING EFFECTIVENESS means that learners who complete an online program receive educations that represent the distinctive quality of the institution. The goal is that online learning is at least equivalent to learning through the institution's other delivery modes, in particular through its traditional face-to-face, classroom-based instruction. If there is no comparable face-to-face course, then the institution's normative benchmark applies. The learning resources in online courses generally include the same ones to be found in the institution's traditional face-to-face courses—learning media (books, notes, software, CD-ROMs, and so on); faculty who teach the class and are available outside of class; and learners who interact with the faculty and with each other. Because of technology, online courses are usually enhanced by pedagogy that emphasizes active learning and uses resources available online and designed for computer conferencing and presentation. Metrics demonstrate that the quality of learning online is at least as good as the institution provides through its traditional programs as measured by several means—by faculty perception; by outcomes assessments; by career, scholastic and professional achievement surveys and records; by feedback from employers; and by institutionally sustained, evidence-based, participatory inquiry into how well online programs achieve learning objectives. Online learning generally parallels the quality of face-to-face learning with equivalent content, standards, and academic support services. Online curricula are subject to, and thereby receive the same benefits of practice, process, and criteria that the institution applies to traditional forms of instruction.

Key practice areas for learning effectiveness include:

- Assessment
- Course design
- Interaction
- Learning outcomes
- Learning resources
- Pedagogy (e.g., active, constructivist, andragogy, agentive, learning style)
- Student perceptions of learning

These principles of effective online education address learning effectiveness:

- Academic standards for all online programs or courses are the

III. The Quality Framework

same as those for other courses or programs delivered at the institution where they originate.
- Online degrees, certificate programs, and courses are coherent and complete.
- Each program or course of study results in learning appropriate to the rigor and breadth of the degree or certificate awarded.
- Learning in online programs or courses is comparable to learning in programs or courses offered at the campus where they originate.
- The institution has admission/acceptance criteria to assess whether the learner has the background, knowledge and technical skills required for undertaking the course program.
- The institution uses evaluation results for continuous program improvement.
- The program or course provides learners with clear, complete and timely information on the curriculum, course, and degree requirements, nature of faculty/learner interaction, prerequisite technology competencies and skills, technical equipment requirements, availability of academic support services, financial aid resources, costs, and payment policies.
- The course or program provides for interaction between faculty and learners and among learners that is both quantitatively and qualitatively sufficient to support course objectives and that is in accordance with the pedagogy and subject matter of the course. Interaction encourages critical thinking, problem solving, analysis, integration and synthesis, as defined in the course objectives.
- Qualified faculty supervise the online program or course, as they do for other modes of instruction.

COST EFFECTIVENESS enables institutions to offer their best educational value to learners. Online programs are regionally accredited (and otherwise as applicable) in the same way as on-campus courses and, generally, online courses are part of a complete degree or certificate program. Institutional commitment to quality and finite resources require continuous improvement policies for developing and assessing cost-effectiveness measures and practices. The goal is to control costs so that tuition is affordable yet sufficient to meet development and maintenance costs—and to provide a return on investment in startup and infrastructure.

Metrics may compare the costs and benefits of delivery modes by discipline and educational level; faculty salary and workload; capital, physical plant, and maintenance investments; equipment and communications technology costs; scalability options; and/or various learning processes and outcomes, such as satisfaction levels and retention rates. These types of comparisons enable institutions to: develop better strategic plans for market demand and capture; achieve capacity enrollment; develop brand recognition; and secure long-term loyalty among current and prospective constituents. Cost-effective practices help to leverage key educational resources while offering new online learning opportunities to students and faculty.

Key practice areas for cost effectiveness include:

- Infrastructure
- Institutional commitment
- Marketing
- Methods for conserving costs, time, effort
- Partnerships
- Scalability

These principles of effective online education address cost effectiveness:

- The program or course is consistent with the institution's role and mission, and with institutional purpose expanding beyond its traditional venues.
- Advertising, recruiting, and admissions materials clearly and accurately represent the program and its services.
- Review and approval processes based on research, experimentation, and continuous improvement ensure the appropriate technology meets program or course objectives.
- The institution demonstrates a commitment to ongoing support, both financial and technical, for the continuation of the program or course for a period sufficient for students to complete a degree or certificate.

ACCESS provides the means for all qualified, motivated students to complete courses, degrees, or programs in their disciplines of choice. The goal is to provide meaningful and effective access throughout the entire student 'life cycle.' Access starts with enabling prospective learners to become aware of available opportunities through effective marketing, branding, and basic program information. It continues with providing program access (e.g., quantity and variety of available program options, clear program information), seamless access to courses (e.g., readiness assessment, intuitive navigability), and appropriate learning resources. Access includes three areas of support: academic (such as tutoring, advising, and library); administrative (such as financial aid, and disability support); and technical (such as hardware reliability and uptime, and help desk). Effective practices for measuring increasing accessibility may analyze and apply the results student and provider surveys, narrative or case study

III. The Quality Framework

description, focus groups, or other means of measuring access. Larger-scale access implementation may also result from mission-based strategic planning in a variety of institutional areas.

Key practice areas for access include:

- Academic and administrative services
- Course access (e.g., course information, readiness assessment)
- Faculty support services
- Learning resources
- Program access (e.g., basic program information, marketing)
- Program offerings (variety of available program options)
- Technical infrastructure

These principles of effective online education address access:

- The program or course documents and evaluates the adequacy of access to learning resources and the cost to learners for access to those resources.
- Enrolled students have reasonable and adequate access to support services and learning resources. The program or course ensures that appropriate learning resources are available to learners. The program or course provides for appropriate interaction between faculty and learners and among learners.
- Review and approval processes ensure the appropriateness of the technology used for meeting program or course objectives.

Just as access can motivate learners, unreliable access can demotivate them.

Access includes support services for:

- Admissions and registration
- Academic advising
- Technical support services (online and in person help)
- Server/portal access
- Rapid textbooks/learning materials delivery or exchange
- Learning resource services and library
- Degree/program mentoring
- Standards of progress tracking
- Readiness and aptitude testing
- Tutoring
- Testing, exam proctoring
- Financial aid
- Career advising and placement

Pillar Reference Manual

- Commencement
- Alumni

FACULTY SATISFACTION means that instructors find the online teaching experience personally rewarding and professionally beneficial. Personal factors contributing to faculty satisfaction with the online experience include opportunities to extend interactive learning communities to new populations of students and to conduct and publish research related to online teaching and learning. Institutional factors related to faculty satisfaction include three categories: support, rewards, and institutional study/research. Faculty satisfaction is enhanced when the institution supports faculty members with a robust and well-maintained technical infrastructure, training in online instructional skills, and ongoing technical and administrative assistance. Faculty members also expect to be included in the governance and quality assurance of online programs, especially as these relate to curricular decisions and development of policies of particular importance to the online environment (such as intellectual property, copyright, royalties, collaborative design, and delivery). Faculty satisfaction is closely related to an institutional reward system that recognizes the rigor and value of online teaching. Satisfaction increases when workload assignments and assessments reflect the greater time commitment in developing and teaching online courses and when online teaching is valued on par with face-to-face teaching in promotion and tenure decisions. A final institutional factor—crucial to recruiting, retaining, and expanding a dedicated online faculty—is commitment to ongoing study of and enhancement of the online faculty experience.

Key practice areas for faculty satisfaction include:

- Access to new populations of students
- Administrative support
- Governance and quality control
- Institutional research on faculty experience
- Institutional rewards
- Opportunities for research and publication
- Participation in interactive learning communities
- Technical infrastructure for instruction
- Technical support (ongoing)
- Technical training in online instruction skills

These principles of effective online education address faculty satisfaction:

- The institution provides faculty support services and training specifically related to teaching online.
- The institution provides faculty with adequate equipment, software and communications for interaction with students,

III. The Quality Framework

institutions and other faculty.
- The course or program provides for appropriate interaction between faculty and students and among students.
- Qualified faculty provide appropriate supervision and control of online programs and courses.
- Policies for faculty evaluation include appropriate recognition of teaching and scholarly activities related to programs or courses offered electronically.

STUDENT SATISFACTION is the most important key to continuing lifelong learning. It reflects learners' evaluation of the quality of all aspects of the educational program. The goal is that all learners who complete online courses with the same institution express satisfaction with course quality, with faculty and peer interaction, and with support services. Online learners put a primary value on constructive, substantive interaction with faculty, and, as appropriate, with classmates in classes that are the same size as equivalent face-to-face classes and are taught by the same kind of faculty. People-to-people interaction is key to constructive learning; so online programs engage distributed learning cohorts. Hence, online programs include asynchronous interaction in media such as email, chats, boards, stored voice, archives, and so on. Occasionally, synchronous interactions may occur. Typically, courses define starting and ending dates in an academic calendar. Learners appreciate faculty who help them think creatively, change opinions and sharpen analyses, and encourage them to take responsibility for their own learning by helping them plan and produce meaningful work through active, authentic, agentive course design. As consumers, learners are satisfied when program information and institutional services—including feedback, tutorials, learning resources, advising, mentoring, testing, readiness and career placement, grade and transfer credit and transcript reporting, degree conferrals, and technologies—are clear, responsive, timely, easily accessible, and relevant to personal and professional goals. Metrics may analyze and apply the results of student and alumni surveys, referrals, testimonials and bequests as measures of perceived satisfaction with institutional quality.

Key practice areas show that students are satisfied with:

- Academic and administrative services
- Appropriateness of technologies
- Interaction with faculty
- Interaction with students
- Learning outcomes that match course description
- Learning community involvement
- Technical support

- Unexpected learning outcomes

These principles of effective online education address student satisfaction:

- Advertising, recruiting and admissions materials clearly and accurately represent the program and the services available.
- Program or course announcements and electronic catalog entries provide appropriate information.
- The institution has admission/acceptance criteria to assess whether the student has the background, knowledge, and technical skills required for undertaking the course program.
- The program or course provides students with clear, complete and timely information on the curriculum, course and degree requirements, nature of faculty/student interaction, prerequisite technology competencies and skills, technical equipment requirements, availability of academic support services, financial aid resources, costs, and payment policies.
- The institution evaluates program and course effectiveness, including student satisfaction.
- At the completion of the program or course, the institution provides for assessment and documentation of student achievement in each course.

Table 3: Learning Effectiveness

Learning Effectiveness		
The provider demonstrates that the quality of learning online is at least as good as the quality of its traditional programs.		
Process/Practice	**Metric**	**Progress Indexes**
Online courses are designed to be equivalent to on-campus courses or to the institutional norm.	The same or similar assessments are used in both modes: For example, formative and summative assessments, pre-tests and post-tests, mid-term and end of course learning assessments, exams, learner/graduate/employer focus groups or sampled interviews; exit exams, licensure, national standard tests (MFAT, PT).	Direct assessment of student learning shows equivalent or better outcomes. Perceptions of learning are equivalent in both modes.

III. The Quality Framework

	Blind review portfolio or coursework assessment. Comparative analyses of faculty/learner/graduate/employer surveys; focus groups or sampled interviews; grade comparisons for eArmyU students with non-eArmyU students in same course, same teacher; achievement test results compared in both modes.	
Academic outcomes and retention/completion rates are compared, measured and continuously improve. Student readiness for online learning is effectively assessed.	Analysis of learning outcomes. Analysis of reasons for withdrawal. Analysis of: Number of and percentage of courses requiring assessment/ placement tests Comparative attrition rates of those who did/not complete assessment/placement tests# Help desk calls # Calls to help desk from students who passed placement assessmentSuccess rates in prior and subsequent courses Tutoring demand and success ratesPercentage of students who pass with C or better grade.	Persistence, completion and retention rates correspond favorably with face-to-face completion rates; success rates continuously improve.
Comprehensive information is available to students prior to enrolling.	Syllabi, reading lists, time-on-task estimates and prior survey results are available during pre-registration.	

| Online courses include interactive and active learning strategies personalized for individual learning styles. | Course syllabi include active learning and interactive pedagogy.

Extent of activity within courses.

Number of postings to course.

Number of interactions, average response time.

Times between logons.

Quality of archived discussions compared with face-to-face interaction.

Quality of online team projects and presentations compared with face-to-face teams and presentations. | Increasing percentage of courses contain active learning strategies. |

Table 4: Cost Effectiveness

Cost Effectiveness		
The provider demonstrates that the quality of learning online is at least as good as the quality of its traditional programs.		
Process/Practice	**Metric**	**Progress Indexes**
Online courses are designed to be equivalent to on-campus courses or to the institutional norm.	The same or similar assessments are used in both modes: For example, formative and summative assessments, pre-tests and post-tests, mid-term and end of course learning assessments, exams, learner/graduate/employer focus groups or sampled interviews; exit exams, licensure, national standard tests (MFAT, PT).	Direct assessment of student learning shows equivalent or better outcomes. Perceptions of learning are equivalent in both modes.

III. The Quality Framework

The institution demonstrates financial and technical commitment to its online programs.	A compelling, active, regularly updated business plan includes benchmarks, constraint analyses, fixed/variable costs, projected income ratios per program, in/direct costs, capacity management, and scalability plans.	
The institution continuously seeks ways to lower costs and improve quality of course development, course delivery, infrastructure and administrative processes.	Expense categories and accountability for implementation and tracking are clear. Cost model ($ return to faculty, department, institution, cost per credit hour, cost per student). Investment costs, e.g. course development, are controlled and recoveredInstitution devotes assets (faculty, administrators, technology infrastructure, etc.) to sustain growing programs. Return on investment, e.g. Internal Rate of Return or Net Present Value analysis.	
The institution adopts an activity-based business plan (private) broken out to the course level. The business plan includes market analysis and risk capital for investments in continuously improving the pedagogical gain-to-cost ratio.	Cost-effective innovations and practices are adopted, e.g., percentage of access and materials online and percentage of access and material offline. Markets are analyzed, defined, and evaluated for new learning demands and return on investment. The institution maintains or increases levels of participation; learners complete degree programs.	

Pillar Reference Manual

The institution prices courses and programs to provide best value to learners and to offset institutional development and delivery costs (See http://www.wiche.edu/telecom/projects/tcm/ for an example cost model).	Enrollments meet institution's projections. As enrollment increases, cost per credit hour decreases.	
Course offerings are designed to be scalable and sustainable to meet anticipated demands.	Technology expenditures are based on studies of effectiveness, flexibility, ease of use, pedagogical and satisfaction impacts, and scalability.	
Tuition rates provide a fair return to the institution and best value to learners at the same time.		
Tuition rates are equivalent or less than on-campus tuition.	Investments are managed to have satisfactory return over time, e.g., upfront costs of curriculum development and institutional infrastructure.	

Table 5: Access

Access		
All learners who wish to learn online can access learning in a wide array of programs and courses.		
Process/Practice	**Metric**	**Progress Indexes**
Program Entry: Processes inform learners of opportunities, and ensure that qualified, motivated learners have reliable access.	Administrative and technical infrastructure provides access to all prospective and enrolled learners. Online training makes users aware of portal features and resources.	Qualitative indicators show continuous improvement in growth and effectiveness. ISP/POP, courseware accessible 99.9% of time and enable rapid up/downloads.

III. The Quality Framework

Student Support Services: Integrated support services are available online to learners.	All services, including admissions, library, registration, advising, bookstore, tutoring, financial aid, career services, academic and administrative policies, IT support, help desk, etc., are accessible online 24x7 and do not require physical presence. Metrics regularly evaluated efficiencies.	# Complaints decline; % satisfaction rises. Admission/Transfer credit evaluation/Student Agreements issued within # days. Incomplete grade advising within # days. Reliable, timely information and delivery of learning materials within # days of registration.
Technical Infrastructure: Technical infrastructure, including physical plant, staffing and technical assistance assures maintenance and expansion of program offerings.	One password enables access to services and courses. Quality metrics regularly measure information dissemination; clarity of information; ease of navigation (#clicks >4, #seconds >10); learning resources delivery time and usage Web portal content is regularly updated; time studies measure web efficiencies; and feedback about the website is solicited from users. Metrics track: *ISP–POP reliability *Growth of programs *Program capacity as a percentage of known (or estimated) total demand *Program enrollment as a percentage of program capacity *Program enrollment relative to program candidates Comparative retention and completion rates.	Grade reporting within # days. Transcripts within # days. Virtual classroom software accounts. Virtual classroom software availability Unfulfilled demand declines.
Program expansion: Processes assure program expansion while maintaining existing support structure and overall program quality.		
Performance feedback from users is used to improve services, responsiveness and information in each of these areas.		

Pillar Reference Manual

Table 6: Faculty Satisfaction

Faculty Satisfaction		
Faculty are pleased with teaching online, citing appreciation and happiness.		
Process/Practice	**Metric**	**Progress Indexes**
Process to ensure adequate support for faculty in course preparation and course delivery.	Repeat teaching of online courses by individual faculty. Addition of new faculty. Faculty perception surveys, focus groups or interviews compare equity and faculty satisfaction with the volume and kinds of training, access to resources, professional development, advancement opportunities, incentives, rewards, workloads, and technical, academic, and administrative support in both delivery modes. Post-course survey of all faculty about their experiences teaching in online programs, preparation/readiness of students, quality of interaction and learning, quality and level of support services, etc. Results used for improvement. Continuous faculty feedback mechanism.	Data from post-course surveys show continuous improvement: At least <n> percentage of faculty believe the overall online teaching/learning experience is positive. Willingness/desire to teach additional courses in the program: <n> percentage positive. Faculty report services for students are appropriately integrated: <n> percentage positive. Faculty report understanding of online preparation, support, and delivery: <n> percentage positive. <n> percentage Participation in training, orientation program and in continuing information dissemination. Faculty regard rewards and incentives as equivalent and satisfactory.
Institutional policies and procedures communicate reliable information to participating faculty.		
Policies clearly communicate expectations, rights, and responsibilities regarding compensation, intellectual property, peer review, tenure and promotion, and contracts.		
Academic integrity and control reside with faculty in the same way as for traditional programs at the institution.		
Online faculty have equivalent inputs to learning process (e.g., faculty mix, student attainment, class size, cohorts).		
Faculty give input into the integration of support services for online students to ensure comparability with services for face to face students.		
Participation in faculty orientation in person, online, or via CD.		

III. The Quality Framework

Table 7: Student Satisfaction

Student Satisfaction		
Students are pleased with their experiences in learning online, including interaction with instructors and peers, learning outcomes that match expectations, services, and orientation.		
Process/Practice	Metric	Progress Indexes
Faculty/learner interaction is timely and substantive.	Summative and normative student surveys, focus groups and/or interviews.	Satisfaction measures show continuously increasing improvement.
Adequate and fair systems assess course learning objectives; results are used for improving learning.	Outcomes measures. Focus groups.	Institutional surveys, interviews, and/or other metrics show satisfaction levels are equivalent to or better than those of other delivery modes for the institution Interaction items on learner surveys evidence continuing improvement. Course evaluation items on learner surveys evidence continuing improvement.
Courses are appropriately rigorous, fair, and effective in supporting learning.		
Learners are given realistic estimates about outcomes, expectations, procedures, and time and effort commitments.	Faculty/Mentor/Advisor/Employer perceptions. Studies correlating interaction and community building with learning effectiveness and satisfaction.	
Learners receive individualized professional guidance with their academic and professional goals, which may include online portfolio preparation.	Alumni and employer surveys, referrals, testimonials.	Declining drop out rates; successful entry into job market, continuing studies, lifelong learning.

Pillar Reference Manual

Appendix A: Pillar Reference Quick Guide

Learning Effectiveness

The provider demonstrates that the quality of learning online is comparable to the quality of its traditional programs:
- ° Interaction is key: with instructors, classmates, the interface, and through vicarious interaction.
- ° Metrics are used for comparing online and traditional courses.
- ° Online course design takes advantage of capabilities of the medium to improve learning (testing, discussion, materials).
- ° Courses are instructor-led.
- ° Communications and community building are emphasized.
- ° Swift trust characterizes the online learning community.
- ° Distinctive characteristics of programs are highlighted to demonstrate improved learning.
- ° On-campus and online instruction achieve comparable learning outcomes, and the institution ensures the quality of learning in both modes by tracking instructional methods, student constituencies and class size.

Cost Effectiveness

Institutions continuously improve services while reducing cost:
- ° Cost-effectiveness models are tuned to institutional goals.
- ° Tuition and fees reflect cost of services delivery.
- ° Scalability, if an institutional objective, can be accommodated.
- ° Partnering and resource sharing are institutional strategies for reducing costs.
- ° Mission-based strategies for cost reduction are continuously formulated and tested.
- ° Intellectual property policies encourage cost effective strategies.

Access

All learners who wish to learn online have the opportunity and can achieve success:
- ° Diverse learning abilities are provided for (e.g., at-risk, disabled, and expert learners).
- ° The reliability and functionality of delivery mechanisms are continuously evaluated.

- Learner-centered courseware is provided.
- Feedback from learners is taken seriously and used for continuous improvement.
- Courses that students want are available when they want them.
- Connectivity to multiple opportunities for learning and service is provided.

Faculty Satisfaction

Faculty achieve success with teaching online, citing appreciation and happiness:

- Faculty satisfaction metrics show improvement over time.
- Faculty contribute to and benefit from online teaching.
- Faculty are rewarded for teaching online and for conducting research about improving teaching online.
- Sharing of faculty experiences, practices, and knowledge about online learning is part of the institutional knowledge sharing structure.
- There is parity in workload between classroom and online teaching.
- Significant technical support and training are provided by the institution.

Student Satisfaction

Students are successful in learning online and are typically pleased with their experiences. Measurement of student attitudes finds that:

- Discussion and interaction with instructors and peers is satisfactory.
- Actual learning experiences match expectations.
- Satisfaction that services (e.g., advising, registration, access to materials) are at least as good as on the traditional campus.
- Orientation for how to learn online is satisfactory.
- Outcomes are useful for career, professional and academic development.

Appendix B: Effective Practices

At a workshop called "Building the Quality Framework" in November 2001, representatives from more than twenty institutions collaborated to identify effective practices and metrics in each of the five pillars. Recognizing that many more effective practices and metrics can be shared, the participants share some workshop results, summarized in the following tables.

Thanks to the people who shared their ideas: Mary Barnes, Anne Arundel Community College; Bart Daig, Baker College; Suzette Chapman, Central Texas Community College; Jay Gould, Defense Acquisition University; Terry Whittum, Embry-Riddle Aeronautical University; Meredyth A. Leahy, Excelsior College; Linda Kick, Franklin University; Kimberly Scott, Lansing Community College; Don Estler, NC A&T State University; Darla Runyon, Northwest Missouri State; Roger Von Holzen, Northwest Missouri State; June Kletzel, Nova Southeastern University; Stephanie Zedlar, Nova Southeastern University; Tony Trippe, University of Phoenix and Rochester Institute of Technology; Gary Miller, Penn State World Campus; Melody Thompson, Penn State World Campus; Karen Mills, Rio Salado Community College; Paul Cochrane, Saint Joseph's College of Maine; Lynn Robinson, Saint Joseph's College of Maine; Marci Goldstein, Saint Leo University; Michael Rogich, Saint Leo University; Jennifer Sheldon, Saint Leo University; Meg Benke, SUNY Empire State College; Linda Frank, SUNY Empire State College; Louis Martini, Thomas Edison State College; Henry van Zyl, Thomas Edison State College; David White, Troy State University; Donna Darling, Troy State University; Sherri Davis, Troy State University; Tricia Hovis, Troy State University; Manfred Meine, Troy State University; Michael Moore, University of Texas at Arlington; Cyndi Wilson Porter, University of the Incarnate Word; Laird Hartman, Utah State University; Vincent Lafferty, Utah State University; Kevin Reeve, Utah State University; George McFarley, Jr., Director of Student Services, Fort Bragg and Pope AFB; Dian Stoskopf, ACES; Judy Brown, ADL Co-Lab; Janet Poley, American Distance Education Consortium; Diana Oblinger, Educause; Alex Ramirez, Hispanic Association of Colleges and Universities; Hank Valentine, Historically Black Colleges and Universities; Paul Stemmer, MIVU; Steve Kime, SOC; Kathy Snead, SOCAD; Bruce Chaloux, Southern Regional Electronic Board; Susan Johnson, US Army; Sally Johnstone, Western Cooperative For Education Telecommunications. From PricewaterhouseCoopers: Amy Baker; Dennis Bundy; Linda Crocker; Andrew Fairbanks; Jeff Carpenter; Kerri Stevens; Amy Baker; Jill Kidwell. From the Sloan Foundation, the Sloan Consortium, and the Sloan Center for Online Education: John Bourne, Mohamad Al-harthi, Martine Dawant, Kathryn Fife, Frank Mayadas, Jim McMichael, Janet Moore, Burks Oakley, Marjorie Quinlan, Jeff Seaman, and John Sener.

Table 8: Learning Effectiveness Practices

Learning Effectiveness
Before the course:
Assess student readiness before course, using check sheet, self-test, sample course. Require orientation as a pre-requisite for taking online courses. Ensure grading standards are consistent across all courses. Provide skills building courses. Make pre- and post-tests available online. Open the doors early; make detailed syllabuses including assignments and estimated time on tasks viewable before course starts. Use constructivist learning principles in course design, moving from what learners know to what they want to learn and beyond. Design courses to construct, not just transmit, knowledge. Make the online curriculum student-centered and personalized; use the 7 principles of good practice (http://www.aahe.org/technology/ehrmann.htm).
During the course:
Specify learning objectives. Communicate high expectations for learning and performance. Make responsibilities clear. Use content maps for students and faculty. Conduct introductions; establish trust and social presence at the beginning of course. Foreground active learning as a predominant feature of online course. Complement learning styles with teaching style. sBalance solitary and group learningInclude real-world, offline learning activities to enhance course relevance. Provide methods for facilitating netiquette and online discussions. Facilitate cohort peer-to-peer learning. Build learning communities. Map content for students and faculty. Use modules that are available from libraries for use in courses (e.g., Merlot). Employ online student portfolios to store work, degree plans, advising, exit exams. Automate techniques to reduce work, e.g.. knowbots, grade reports, test scores, automatic receipts, reminder messages. Use non-graded, self-tests and quizzes to reinforce learning. Create course components to fit asynchronous/synchronous tradeoffs. Use pre- and post-tests to demonstrate achievement.
Quality improvement:
Make using evaluation results to revise courses a priority. Measure learning outcomes. Compare learning outcomes online with learning on-ground. Measure the quantity and quality of student/faculty and student/student interaction and responsiveness. Survey alumni, grad schools, and employers for program and learning effectiveness. Evaluate the impact of online pedagogy on in-class pedagogy.

Appendix B: Effective Practices

Table 9: Cost Effectiveness Practices

Cost Effectiveness
Before implementation:
Create a business plan for delivering online courses, including start-up and fixed costs and expected returns. Optimize the business model to create return to institutions. Strategize the overall institutional plan to include plans for online learning programs. The institution is committed to online learning and provides resources for it. The institution articulates how online programs support its mission. The institution conducts SWOT market analyses. The institution plans for capacity enrollment. The institution plans for faculty growth. The institution plans for technological infrastructure.
Cost efficiencies:
Automate everything that can be automated, e.g., information in FAQ. Put all information online to reduce costs of mailing and duplicating materials. Reduce the number of course management systems for cost effectiveness. Encourage peer-to-peer learning as a way to save faculty time. Use graduate students and teaching assistants as facilitators. Use staff facilitators to reduce faculty time. Make faculty compensation consistent with compensation for on-campus courses, with consideration of comparable workloads. Base faculty compensation on enrollment. Use flexible start dates to enable classes to continue that could be cancelled due to enrollment caps. Share courses across schools; use free courseware and learning objects. Use and share courses with other institutions to reduce course development time. Use materials from publishers to reduce materials cost.
Planning for growth:
Specify relationship between quality and costs. Compare per credit costs and charges online and on-campus; aim for consistent tuition and fees in both modes. Include indirect costs in analyses of spending and results. Design strategic partnerships to reduce course development time. Regularly re-evaluate plans for scaling up.

Pillar Reference Manual

Table 10: Access Practices

Access
Program/course entry:
Provide information to students in advance of the course to eliminate the fear factor. From the start, create a comfort level with technology. Include mandatory orientation/training, i.e., library supported by instructors. Open "class doors" early to familiarize students with environment and help to estimate time on task. Instructors communicate course structure to students. Communicate the roles and responsibilities of faculty and students at the beginning of each course. Use rolling admissions and continuous enrollment to expand access.
Support services:
Provide equivalent access to student services for students on-campus and on-line. Create a web site with all relevant information and links specifically for soldier-students (NSU). Enable toll-free access to help desk/student support available online/phone. Employ student mentors and ambassadors to help online students. Provide anytime-anywhere access to support (tutors), e.g., "beep a tutor." Enable online access to application, registration, orientation, and scheduling. Provide online access to library databases and resources, writers complex writing lab, tutor contact information, secure student records (with password), and full text library services. Build learning community with access to the complete university environment (services, library, art works, etc, newspaper, career services). Accommodate time-zone differences.
Technical infrastructure:
Make learning management systems reliable; 24x7 availability; backup services provided. Accessibility and content of web sites are continuously monitored (www.macromedia.com/accessibility; www.cast.org/bobby). Streamline navigability, reduce number of clicks to destination, provide quick links for students. Use single password for all access. Offer ISP reimbursement for faculty. Provide faculty with necessary equipment to access courses: make it easy. Provide additional servers as demand increases. Make contingency plans for disasters. Program expansion:Conduct needs/desires assessments with current and prospective students (see 2-Minute Advisor). Increase the breadth of course offerings by collaborating with others. Continuously work to expand access to students not served. Provide services through a consolidator (such as eArmyU).

Appendix B: Effective Practices

Table 11: Faculty Satisfaction Practices

Faculty Satisfaction
Rights and responsibilities:
Faculty govern online program and courses curriculum content, sequence, design, delivery, assessment, and improvement, as they do for on campus instruction. Faculty use outcomes and evaluation results to improve learning. Faculty develop learning outcomes and curricula. Robust course management systems are provided and maintained without faculty needing to do anything.
Support:
The administration supports teaching online. Support staff help faculty. Clarify in written institutional policy the relationship between teaching and research for promotion. Provide a faculty policies website for teaching online. Clarify intellectual property policies in writing. Enable faculty to experience the online environment as students experience it. Increase comfort with technology through seminars, continuous training, incentives. Give faculty certificates and credit for professional development for training to teach online courses. Provide peer assessment of courses. Set response time standards, e.g., 24 hours for acknowledgement, 3 days for grades. Establish optimal class sizes. Actively seek innovations to save faculty time. Ways to minimize email overload (FAQs, bulletin boards, listservs, virtual office hours) are established. Ways to use and share the pedagogical advantages of internet. Ways to enhance learner motivation are shared, e.g., guest lecturers, discussion archives, student web pages, knowledge management systems, webliographies, multiple peer review, and longitudinal assessment.
Benefits:
Faculty can secure tenure and promotion through online activities. Compensation for developing courses is provided to faculty Incentives recognize greater time commitment for teaching online. Faculty receive additional money for teaching online. Faculty receive release time for teaching online. Faculty are certified as trained, online teachers. Faculty mentors and peer assessment are available; faculty exchange best practices. Faculty engage in discussion forums and faculty meetings. Regular input from faculty is used to improve teaching and learning. Online and in-class faculty sustain collegiality and integrate effective methods. Ensure that a high percentage of faculty institution-wide believe online pedagogy is effective and beneficial. Emphasize that online learning can turn teaching into publication and presentation.

Table 12: Student Satisfaction Practices

Student Satisfaction
For prospective and beginning learners:
24-hour online academic advising is available (from outside vendor).   24x7 help desk is toll free.   Toll free call center available.   A comparison of courses (online vs. on-ground) is available to students.   Before enrolling, students can view eBay style course reviews and testimonials by other students.   A common course platform look and feel helps students taking courses from the same or different campuses.
After enrollment:
Each student receives a welcome letter.   Student orientation online is available.   Software orientation is available.   A wide range of services offered in a timely and personalized manner.   Staff serve as ombudsmen for students.   Mentors are assigned to each student.   Student expectations are set at the outset of each course; printed publications help set expectations.   Student-to-student interaction is provided.   Instructors stimulate learning, effective communication, and critical thinking.   Formative and normative surveys are continuously accessible so that issues may be addressed immediately.   Evaluations are categorized to get specific views (course content differentiated from instructor evaluations).   Courses are matched to learner readiness and maturity.   Additional instructor support is given at the beginning of the course.   Resources are provided at the outset: access to tech support, phone numbers.   Books and course materials are received in a timely manner.   eBay style reviews are viewable for enrolling students who wish to hear what their colleagues think when they are deciding which courses to take.   Use non-linear learning to help students to pursue their own interests, personalizing their educations.   Building learning communities is an institutional priority.
After completion:
Encourage graduates to maintain affiliation in learning community.   Provide networking opportunities.   Follow with longitudinal studies and surveys.   Provide continuing placement services.   Offer lifelong learning.   Maintain affiliation with graduates.

Appendix C: References (alphabetized)

ADEC Courseware Tools: http://www.adec.edu/courseware.html
Advanced Distributed Learning Network: http://www.adlnet.org/
Advance Distributed Learning Network Co Lab. http://www.wiadlcolab.org/
American Association for History and Computing. Guidelines for Evaluating Digital Media Activities in Tenure, Review, and Promotion. October 2001. http://www.theaahc.org/tenure_guidelines.htm
American Association of University Professors. "Statement on Distance Education." 1999. http://www.aaup.org/govrel/distlern/spcdistn.htm
American Council of Education. Academic Excellence and Cost Management National Awards Program: http://www.acenet.edu/about/programs/programs&analysis/policy&analysis/cost-awards/
Andriole, S. "Requirements-Driven ALN Course Design, Development, Delivery & Evaluation." *Journal of Asynchronous Learning Networks.* JALN, Volume 1, Issue 2. August 1997. http://www.aln.org/alnweb/journal/issue2/andriole.htm
Arp, B. "Increasing the Effectiveness of Online Education through Personalization." http://www.ipfw.edu/as/tohe/2001/Papers/moseley.htm
Arvan, L. "An Introduction to Faculty Satisfaction." In *Online Education, Volume 1.* Needham, MA: Sloan-C, 2000. *Journal of Asynchronous Learning Networks.* JALN, Volume 4, Issue 3. September 2000. http://www.aln.org/alnweb/journal/jaln-vol4issue3.htm
Arvan, L. The Excelets Page. http://edtech3.cet.uiuc.edu/l-arvan/ExceletsWeb/ExceletsHome.htm
Beaudin, B. "Keeping Online Asynchronous Discussions on Topic." *Journal of Asynchronous Learning Networks.* JALN, Volume 3: Issue 2. http://www.aln.org/alnweb/journal/Vol3_issue2
Berg, G. "Early Patterns of Faculty Compensation for Developing and Teaching Distance Learning Courses." *Journal of Asynchronous Learning Networks.* JALN, Volume 4, Issue 1. June 2000. http://www.aln.org/alnweb/journal/Vol4_issue1/berg.htm
Bishop, T., SchWeber, C. "UMUC's Online MBA Program: A Case Study of Cost Effectiveness and the Implications for Large-scale Programs." In *Online Education, Volume 2 in the Sloan-C™ Series.* Needham, MA: Sloan-C, 2001.
Bishop, T., SchWeber, C. "Linking Quality and Cost." In *Elements of Quality Online Education: Volume 3 in the Sloan-C™ Series.* Needham, MA: Sloan-C, 2002.
Blum, K. "Gender Differences in Asynchronous Learning in Higher Education: Learning Styles, Participation Barriers and Communication

Patterns." *Journal of Asynchronous Learning Networks.* JALN, Volume 3, Issue 1. May 1999. http://aln.org/alnweb/journal/Vol3_issue1/blum.htm

Bobby Approval: http://www.cast.org/bobby/

Bourne, J. "Net-Learning*: Strategies for On-Campus and Off-Campus Network-enabled Learning." *Journal of Asynchronous Learning Networks.* JALN, Volume 2, Issue 2. September 98. http://www.aln.org/alnweb/journal/vol2_issue2/bourne2.htm

Bourne, J., Brodersen, A., Campbell, J., Dawant, M. Shiavi, R. "A Model of Online Learning Networks in Engineering Education." *Journal of Asynchronous Learning Networks.* JALN, Volume 1, Issue 1. March 1997. http://www.aln.org/alnweb/jounral/issue1/bourne.htm

Bradburn, E. Distance Education Instruction by Postsecondary Faculty and Staff: Fall 1998. http://nces.ed.gov/pubsearch/pubsinfo.asp?pubid=2002155

Bransford, J., Brown, A. L., Cocking, R.R., Eds. *How People Learn: Brain, Mind, Experience, and School: Expanded Edition.* Washington, D.C.: National Academy Press, 2000. http://www.nap.edu/books/0309070368/html/

Brown, R.E. "The Process of Building Community in Distance Learning Classes." *Journal of Asynchronous Learning Networks.* JALN, Volume 5: Issue 2. http://www.aln.org/alnweb/journal/Vol5_issue2

Campbell, O. "Factors In ALN Cost Effectiveness at BYU." In *Elements of Quality Online Education: Volume 3 in the Sloan-C™ Series.* Needham, MA: Sloan-C, 2002.

Campos, M., Laferrière, T., Harasim, L. "The Post-Secondary Networked Classroom: Renewal of Teaching Practices and Social Interaction." *Journal of Asynchronous Learning Networks.* JALN, Volume 5: Issue 2. http://www.aln.org/alnweb/journal/Vol5_Issue2

Carr, S. "As Distance Education Comes of Age, the Challenge Is Keeping the Students." *The Chronicle of Higher Education.* February 11, 2000. http://chronicle.com/free/v46/i23/23a00101.htm

Carr, S. "Is Anyone Making Money on Distance Education?" *The Chronicle of Higher Education.* February 16, 2001.

Centre for Curriculum, Transfer and Technology: http://www.c2t2.ca

Chickering, A., Ehrmann, S. "Implementing the Seven Principles: Technology as Lever." http://www.aahe.org/technology/ehrmann.htm

Collaborative Digital Reference Service, http://www.loc.gov/rr/digiref

Coppola, N., Hiltz, S. R., Rotter, N. "The Effective Digital Socrates: Developing Trust in Virtual Learning Communities." Presentation at the 6th Annual Sloan ALN Conference, November 2001.

Crumpton Curriculum Design Concept Map. http://lmu.uce.ac.uk/crumpton/curriculum-design.htm

de Castell, S., Bryson, M., Jenson, J. "Object Lessons: Towards an *Educational* Theory of Technology." *First Monday.* Volume 7, Number 1 - January 7 2002. http://www.firstmonday.dk/issues/issue7_1/index.html

Appendix C: References (alphabetized)

Dede, C. "Distance Learning to Distributed Learning: Making the Transition." Reprinted with permission from Learning & Leading with Technology, vol. 23 no. 7, pp. 25-30, copyright (c) 1996, ISTE (International Society for Technology in Education): http://www.educause.edu/nlii/articles/dede.html

DiBiase, D. "Using e-Portfolios at Penn State to Enhance Student Learning: Status, Prospects, and Strategies." February 16, 2002. http://www.e-education.psu.edu/portfolios/e-port_report.shtml

DiPaolo, A. Online Education: "The Rise of a New Educational Industry." January 24, 2001. http://scpd.stanford.edu/SCPD/js/brandingFrame/externalURL.htm

Duderstadt, J. "The Future of the University in an Age of Knowledge." *Journal of Asynchronous Learning Networks.* JALN, Volume 1, Issue 2. August 1997. http://www.aln.org/alnweb/journal/issue2/duderstadt.htm

eArmyU. RFP for prospective partners at: http://www.earmyu.com/public/public_about-auao_become-a-partner.asp

Eaton, J. "Core Academic Values, Quality, and Regional Accreditation: The Challenge of Distance Learning." Council for Higher Education Accreditation. Washington, DC. 2000. http://www.chea.org/Research/core-values.cfm

Educause: http://www.educause.edu/ep/

Environmental Education and Training Partnership. EETAP: http://www.eetap.org

Estabrook, L. "Rethinking Cost Benefit Models of Instruction." In *Elements of Quality Online Education: Volume 3 in the Sloan-C™ Series.* Needham, MA: Sloan-C, 2002.

Eustis, J., McMillan, G. "Libraries Address the Challenges of Asynchronous Learning." *Journal of Asynchronous Learning Networks.* JALN, Volume 2, Issue 1, March 1998. http://www.aln.org/alnweb/jounral/vol2_issue1/eustis.htm

Feldberg, J. "Five Insider Secrets to Designing and Developing EFFECTIVE Online Course in Record Time Without a Big Budget." Educational Pathways. January 2002. http://www.edpath.com

Fredericksen, E., Pickett, A., Shea, P., Pelz, W., Swan, K. "Student Satisfaction and Perceived Learning with Online Courses: Principles and Examples from the SUNY Learning Network." In *Online Education, Volume 1.* Needham, MA: Sloan-C, 2002. *Journal of Asynchronous Learning Networks.* JALN, Volume 4, Issue 2. September 2000. http://www.aln.org/alnweb/journal/jaln-volume4issue3.htm

Geith, C., Vignare, K. "Online Degree Programs: Service and Cost" *Online Education: Volume 2.* Needham, MA., Sloan-C, 2001. [Quotation from: Keegan, D. (1980). On Defining Distance Education, Distance Education. Vol. 1, No. 1. P. 13]

Gilbert, S. Low Threshold Applications. http://tc.unl.edu/cansorge/lowthreshold/

Gold, S. "A Constructivist Approach to Online Training for Online Teachers." *Journal of Asynchronous Learning Networks.* JALN, Vol 5: Issue 1. http://www.aln.org/alnweb/journal/jaln-vol5_issue1.htm

Gomory, R. E. "Internet Learning: Is It Real and What Does It Mean for Universities? The Sheffield Lecture, Yale University, January 11, 2000." *Journal of Asynchronous Learning Networks.* JALN, Volume 5, Issue 1. June 2001. http://www.aln.org/alnweb/journal/jaln-vol5issue1.htm#Gomory

Graham, C., Cagiltay, K., Lim, B., Craner, J. and Duffy, T. "Seven Principles of Effective Teaching: A Practical Lens for Evaluating Online Courses." March/April 2001. http://horizon.unc.edu/TS/default.asp?show=article&id=839 and results: http://crlt.indiana.edu/publications/crlt00-13.pdf

Granger, D. & Benke, M. "Supporting Learners at a Distance from Inquiry Through Completion." *Distance Learners in Higher Education: Institutional Responses for Quality Outcomes*, Campbell, C. editor. Gibson. Atwood Publishing, Madison, Wisconsin, 1998.

Graves, W. "Free Trade in Higher Education: The Meta University." *Journal of Asynchronous Learning Networks.* Volume 1, Issue 1. http://www.aln.org/alnweb/journal/issue1/graves.htm

Green, K. *The Chronicle of Higher Education.* "Colloquy Live" discussion on Working with Technology and Winning Tenure. February 20, 2002. http://chronicle.com/colloquylive/2002/02/tenure/chat.php3

Hartman, J., Dziuban, C., Moskal, P. "Faculty Satisfaction in ALNs: A Dependent or Independent Variable?" In *Online Education, Volume 1.* Needham, MA: Sloan-C, 2000. *Journal of Asynchronous Learning Networks.* JALN, Volume 4, Issue 2. September 2000. http://www.aln.org/alnweb/journal/jaln-volume4issue3.htm

Hawisher, G., Pemberton, M. "Writing Across the Curriculum Encounters Asynchronous Learning Networks or WAC Meets Up With ALN." *Journal of Asynchronous Learning Networks.* JALN, Volume 1, Issue 1. March 1997. http://www.aln.org/alnweb/journal/issue1/hawisher.htm

Hiltz, R., Coppola, N., Rotter, N., Turoff, M. "Measuring the Importance of Collaborative Learning for the Effectiveness of ALN: A Multi Measure, Multi-Method Approach." In *Online Education, Volume 1.* Needham, MA: Sloan-C, 2000. *Journal of Asynchronous Learning Networks.* JALN, Volume 4, Issue 2. September 2000. http://www.aln.org/alnweb/journal/jaln-vol4issue2.htm

Hiltz, R., Zhang, Y., Turoff, M. "Studies of Effectiveness of Learning Networks." *Elements of Quality Online Education: Volume 3 in the Sloan-C™ Series.* Needham, MA: Sloan-C, 2002.

Hislop, G. "Operating Cost of an Online Degree Program." In *Online Education, Volume 2.* Needham, MA: Sloan-C, 2001.

Appendix C: References (alphabetized)

IMS Global Learning Consortium, Inc. http://www.imsproject.org/aboutims.html

Jaffee, D. "Institutionalized Resistance To Asynchronous Learning Networks." Journal of Asynchronous Learning Networks. JALN, Volume 2, Issue 2. September 98. http://www.aln.org/alnweb/journal/vol2_issue2/jaffee.htm

Jones, D. *Technology Costing Methodology Project.* WCET and WICHE, March 2001. http://www.wiche.edu/telecom/projects/tcm/TCM_Handbook_Final.pdf

Kashy, E., Thoennessen, M., Alberti, G., Tsai, Y. "Implementing a Large On-Campus ALN: Faculty Perspective." Online Education, Volume 1. Needham, MA: Sloan-C, 2000. *Journal of Asynchronous Learning Networks.* JALN, Volume 4, Issue 2. September 2000. http://www.aln.org/alnweb/journal/jaln-volume4issue3.htm

Keeton, M.T., Scheckley, B.G., Krecji-Griggs, J. *Effectiveness and Efficiency in Higher Education for Adults.* Council on Adult and Experiential Learning. Chicago: Kendall-Hunt, 2002.

Knowledge Media Lab: http://kml2.carnegiefoundation.org/gallery/index.html

Krauth, B., Carbajal, J. Guide to Developing Online Student Services: http://www.wiche.edu/telecom/resources/publications/guide/guide.htm accessed 2/8/02

Latchman, H.A. "Lectures on Demand in ALN: Enhancing the Online Learning Experience." *Journal of Asynchronous Learning Networks.* JALN, Volume 5, Issue 1. June 2001. http://www.aln.org/alnweb/journal/Vol5_issue1/Latchman/Latchman.htm

Lynch, D. "Professors Should Embrace Technology." *The Chronicle of Higher Education.* January 18, 2002. http://chronicle.com/weekly/v48/i19/19b01501.htm

Maryland Online. http://www.mdfaconline.org/

Massachusetts Institute of Technology OpenCourseWare: http://web.mit.edu/ocw

Mayadas, F. "Asynchronous Learning Networks: A Sloan Foundation Perspective." *Journal of Asynchronous Learning Networks.* JALN, Volume 1, Issue 1. March 1997. http://www.aln.org/alnweb/journal/issue1/mayadas.htm

Mayadas F. Adapted from "Testimony to the Kerrey Commission on Web-Based Education." Reprinted in *Journal of Asynchronous Learning Networks.* JALN, Volume 5, Issue 1. June 2001. http://www.aln.org/alnweb/journal/jaln-vol5issue1.htm

McFarlane, F., Baars, A., Stevens, B., Warn, M. "Effectiveness of Distance Education as a Means for Graduate Education - a Study of Two Student Groups." Nd. http://www.distance-educator.com/dailynews/mcfarland_print.htm

McGrath, J., Middleton, H., Crissman, T. "World Campus: Setting Standards in Student Services." In *Elements of Quality Online Education: Volume 3 in the Sloan-C™ Series*. Needham, MA: Sloan-C, 2002.

McNaught, C. "Quality Assurance for Online Courses: Implementing Policy at RMIT." In *Assessment: The Technology Source*. January/February 2002. http://ts.mivu.org/default.asp?show=article&id=940

Merlot: http://www.merlot.org

Miller, G. "Asynchronous Learning Networks and Distance Education: An Interview with Frank Mayadas of the Alfred P. Sloan Foundation." Reprinted on the ALN Web with permission of *The American Journal of Distance Education*, Volume 11, No. 3. http://www.aln.org/alnweb/mayadas_miller.htm

Miller, G. "Penn State's World Campus: A Case Study in Achieving Cost Efficiencies in ALN." In Online *Education, Volume 2*. Needham, MA: Sloan-C, 2001.

Miller, G. Excerpts from Sloan-C™ listserv emails dated January 10 and January 17, 2002.

MIT Open Knowledge Initiative: http://web.mit.edu/oki/

Montessori, M. *The Discovery of the Child.* Oxford, England, Clio Press: 1989. "Actually, he will learn from the child himself the ways and means to his own education, that is, he will learn from the child himself how to perfect himself as a teacher." http://www.moteaco.com/clio/discovery.pdf

Moonen, J. "The Efficiency of Telelearning." *Journal of Asynchronous Learning Networks*. JALN, Volume 1, Issue 2. August 1997. http://www.aln.org/alnweb/journal/issue2/moonen.htm

Moore, M. "Editorial: Is Distance Teaching More Work or Less?" *The American Journal of Distance Education*. Volume 14, Number 3, 2000. http://www.ajde.com/Contents/vol14_3.htm

Morgan, B. Determining the Costs of Online Education. http://webpages.marshall.edu/~morgan16/onlinecosts

National Association of College and University Business Officers. "Explaining College Costs: NACUBO's Methodology For Identifying The Costs of Delivering Undergraduate Education." http://www.nacubo.org/public_policy/cost_of_college/content.html

National Center for Education Statistics. "2001, Condition of Education: Participation in Adult Learning." http://nces.ed.gov/

National Center for Public Policy and Higher Education. "Measuring Up 2000: The State-by-State Report Card for Higher Education." http://measuringup2000.highereducation.org/nationalpicture.htm

Neal, L. "Predictions for 2002." ELearn Magazine. http://www.elearnmag.org/subpage/sub_page.cfm?article_pk=2901&page_number_nb=1&title=COLUMN

Appendix C: References (alphabetized)

Newman, F., Scurry, J. "Online Technology Pushes Pedagogy to the Forefront." *The Chronicle of Higher Education.* July 13, 2001. http://chronicle.com/weekly/v47/i44/44b00701.htm

Occupational Outlook Handbook: http://www.bls.gov/oco/ocos066.htm

"Online Learning: Is It for Me?" http://www.monroecc.edu/depts/distlearn/minicrs/10mythsindex.htm

"Report of the University of Illinois Teaching at an Internet Distance Seminar, December, 1999." http://www.vpaa.uillinois.edu/tid/report/

Pimentel, J. "Design of Net-learning Systems Based on Experiential Learning." *Journal of Asynchronous Learning Networks.* JALN, Volume 3, Issue 2. November 1999. http://www.aln.org/alnweb/journal/Vol3_issue2/pimentel.htm

Reid, I. "Beyond Models: Developing a University Model for Online Instruction." *Journal of Asynchronous Networks.* Volume 3, Issue 1 - May 1999. http://www.aln.org/alnweb/journal/Vol3_issue1/reid.htm

Rockwell, S., Schauer, J., Fritz, S., Marx D. "Incentives and Obstacles Influencing Higher Education Faculty and Administrators to Teach Via Distance." *Online Journal of Distance Learning Administration.* Volume 2, Number 3. Winter 1999. http://www.westga.edu/~distance/rockwell24.html

Rossman, M. "Successful Online Teaching Using An Asynchronous Learner Discussion Forum." *Journal of Asynchronous Learning Networks.* JALN, Volume 3, Issue 2. November 1999. http://www.aln.org/alnweb/journal/Vol3_issue2/Rossman.htm

Ruch, R. *Higher Ed. Inc. The Rise of the For-Profit University.* Baltimore: The Johns Hopkins University Press, 2001:159.

Rumble, G. "The Costs and Costing of Networked Learning." *Journal of Asynchronous Learning Networks.* JALN, Volume 5, Issue 2. September 2001. http://aln.org/alnweb/journal/Vol5_issue2/Rumble/Rumble.htm

Sachs, D., Hale, N. "Pace University's Focus on Student Satisfaction With Student Services in Online Education." In *Elements of Quality Online Education: Volume 3 in the ™ Series.* Needham, MA: Sloan-C, 2002.

Schroeder, R. http://people.uis.edu/rschr1/bloggerinfo.html

Sener, J., Stover, M. ""Integrating ALN into an Independent Study Distance Education Program: NVCC Case Studies." In *Online Education, Volume 1.* Needham, MA: Sloan-C, 2000. *Journal of Asynchronous Learning Networks.* JALN, Volume 4, Issue 3. September 2000. . http://www.aln.org/alnweb/journal/jaln-vol4issue3.htm

Serendip. http://serendip.brynmawr.edu

Shapley, P. "On-line Education to Develop Complex Reasoning Skills in Organic Chemistry." *Journal of Asynchronous Learning Networks.* JALN, Volume 4, Issue 2. September 2000. http://www.aln.org/alnweb/journal/Vol4_issue2/le/shapley/LE-shapley.htm

Shea, P., Pelz, W., Fredericksen, E. and Pickett, A. "Online Teaching as a Catalyst for Classroom-Based Instructional Transformation." In *Elements of*

Quality Online Education: Volume 3 in the Sloan-C™ Series. Needham, MA: Sloan-C, 2002.

Shea, P., Swan, K., Fredericksen, E., Pickett, A. "Student Satisfaction and Reported Learning in the SUNY Learning Network." In *Elements of Quality Online Education: Volume 3 in the ™ Series.* Needham, MA: Sloan-C, 2002.

Sloan-C™ Online Learning Enrollment Survey http://www.sloanconsortium.org/alnenrollments/showdata.cfm

Southern Regional Electronic Board: http://www.evalutech.sreb.org/criteria/web.asp

Staley, A., MacKenzie, N. "Enabling Curriculum Re-design Through Asynchronous Learning Networks." *Journal of Asynchronous Learning Networks.* JALN, Volume 4: Issue 1. http://www.aln.org/alnweb/jounral/Vol4_issue1/staleyMacKenzie.htm

Stokes, P. "CMS Users Still Waiting for the Killer App: Higher Education Institutions Seek Improved Support Services and Greater Integration from Leading Providers of Course Management Systems." Eduventures.com. February 2001. http://www.eduventures.com/research/industry_research_resources/big_bang.cfm

Stokes, P., Evans, T. "After the Big Bang: Higher Education E-Learning Markets Get Set to Consolidate." Eduventures.com: October 2000. http://www.eduventures.com/research/industry_research_resources/big_bang.cfm

Swan, K. "Immediacy, Social Presence, Asynchronous Discussion." In *Elements of Quality Online Education: Volume 3 in the ™ Series.* Needham, MA: Sloan-C, 2002.

Taylor, J. "Virtual Writing Forum With Don Murray and the National Writing Project in an Asynchronous Environment." *Journal of Asynchronous Learning Networks.* JALN, Volume 5: Issue 1. June 2001. http://www.aln.org/alnweb/journal/Vol5_issue1/Taylor/Taylor.htm

Thaiupathump, C., Bourne, J., Campbell, O. "Intelligent Agents for Online Learning." *Journal of Asynchronous Learning Networks.* JALN, Volume 3, Issue 2. November 1999. http://www.aln.org/alnweb/journal/Vol3_issue2/Choon2.htm

The Boyer Commission on Educating Undergraduates in the Research University. "Reinventing Undergraduate Education: A Blueprint for America's Research Universities." Publication Date: 1998. http://naples.cc.sunysb.edu/Pres/boyer.nsf/

The Campus Computing Project. http://www.campuscomputing.net/

The Centre for Curriculum, Transfer & Technology. Online Educational Delivery Applications: A Web Tool for Comparative Analysis. http://www.c2t2.ca/landonline

The Chronicle of Higher Education. "Reliance on Part-Time Faculty Members and How They Are Treated, Selected Disciplines." December 2001. http://chronicle.com/weekly/v47/i14/14a01301.htm. Based on data from the American Historical Association: http://www.theaha.org/caw/index.htm

The Internet Public Library: http://www.ipl.org

The Lincoln Library: http://lincoln.library.uiuc.edu:8000

The Mellon Foundation: "Cost Effective Uses of Technology in Teaching." http://www.ceutt.org/

The National Center for Education Statistics report is available at http://www.nces.ed.gov

The National Survey of Student Engagement. "The College Student Report: Effective Educational Practices, An Untapped Dimension of Quality." NSSE 2000. http://www.indiana.edu/~nsse/acrobat/report-2000.pdf

The Pew Grant Program in Course Redesign Course Planning Tool http://www.center.rpi.edu/PewGrant/Tool.html

The Sloan Consortium Effective Practices: http://www.sloan-c.org/effectivepractices

The Sloan Consortium. "Mission Statement." http://www.sloan-c.org

Thompson, M. "Faculty Satisfaction in Penn State's World Campus." In *Online Education, Volume 2.* Needham, MA: Sloan-C, 2001.

Thompson, M., McGrath, J. "Using ALNs to Support a Complete Educational Experience." *Journal of Asynchronous Learning Networks.* JALN, Volume 3, Issue 2. November 1999. http://www.aln.org/alnweb/journal/jaln-vol3issue2.htm

TLT Group: http://www.tltgroup.org

Trippe, T. "Student Satisfaction at the University of Phoenix Online Campus." In *Elements of Quality Online Education: Volume 3 in the Sloan-C ™ Series.* Needham, MA: Sloan-C, 2002.

Turgeon, A. "Introducing the Penn State World Campus through Certificate Program in Turfgrass Management and Geographic Information Systems." In *Online Education, Volume 1.* Needham, MA: Sloan-C, 2000. *Journal of Asynchronous Learning Networks.* JALN, Volume 4, Issue 3. September 2000. http://www.aln.org/alnweb/journal/Vol4_issue3/fs/turgeon/fs-turgeon.htm

Turoff, M., Hiltz, S.R. "Effectively Managing Large Enrollment Courses: A Case Study." In *Online Education, Volume 2.* Needham, MA: Sloan-C, 2001.

Twigg, C. "Improving Learning and Reducing Costs: Redesigning Large-Enrollment Courses. The Pew Learning and Technology Program." July 1999. http://www.center.rpi.edu/PewSym/mono2.html

Twigg, C. "Innovations in Online Learning: Moving Beyond No Significant Difference." The Pew Learning and Technology Program. December 2000. http://www.center.rpi.edu/PewSym/mono4.html

Twigg, C. "Quality Assurance for Whom? Providers and Consumers in Today's Distributed Learning Environment. " December, 2000. http://www.center.rpi.edu/PewSym/mono3.html

Twigg, C., Heterick, R. "It's Not How Fast You Run." *The Learning MarketSpace*. March 1, 2002. http://www.center.rpi.edu/LForum/LM/Mar02.html

University of Maryland Center for Intellectual Property. http://www.umuc.edu/distance/odell/cip/workshop_ipacademia/faq.html

University of Massachusetts Center for Information Technology and Dispute Resolution. http://www.ombuds.org/course2001/odr101.htm

World Lecture Hall: http://www.utexas.edu/world/lecture

World Wide Web Consortium (W3C) guidelines: http://www.w3.org/WAI/Resources/#gl

Wright, T. Interview with Chris Dede. Syllabus Magazine. June 2002. http://www.syllabus.com/syllabusmagazine/article.asp?id=6388

Young, J. "Ever So Slowly, Colleges Start to Count Work With Technology in Tenure Decisions." *The Chronicle of Higher Education*. February 22, 2002.

Young, J. "Professor Says Distance Education Will Flop Unless Universities Revamp Themselves."
The Chronicle of Higher Education. June 29, 2001.

Appendix D: References (by section)

Introduction

1. Gomory, R. E. "Internet Learning: Is It Real and What Does It Mean for Universities? The Sheffield Lecture, Yale University, January 11, 2000." *Journal of Asynchronous Learning Networks.* JALN, Volume 5, Issue 1. June 2001. http://www.aln.org/alnweb/journal/jaln-vol5issue1.htm#Gomory
2. Mayadas, F. "Asynchronous Learning Networks: A Sloan Foundation Perspective." *Journal of Asynchronous Learning Networks.* JALN, Volume 1, Issue 1. March 1997. http://www.aln.org/alnweb/journal/issue1/mayadas.htm
3. Miller, G. "Asynchronous Learning Networks and Distance Education: An Interview with Frank Mayadas of the Alfred P. Sloan Foundation." Reprinted on the ALN Web with permission of *The American Journal of Distance Education*, Volume 11, No. 3. http://www.aln.org/alnweb/mayadas_miller.htm
4. The Sloan Consortium. "Mission Statement." http://www.sloan-c.org
5. Mayadas F. Adapted from "Testimony to the Kerrey Commission on Web-Based Education." Reprinted in *Journal of Asynchronous Learning Networks.* JALN, Volume 5, Issue 1. June 2001. http://www.aln.org/alnweb/journal/jaln-vol5issue1.htm
6. Ruch, R. *Higher Ed. Inc. The Rise of the For-Profit University.* Baltimore, The Johns Hopkins University Press, 2001:159.

The Pillars: Learning Effectiveness

7. ALN Web Center: Learning Networks Effective Research: http://www.alnresearch.org
8. Hiltz, R., Zhang, Y., Turoff, M. "Studies of Effectiveness of Learning Networks." *Elements of Quality Online Education: Volume 3 in the Sloan-C™ Series.* Needham, MA: Sloan-C, 2002.
9. Dede, C. "Distance Learning to Distributed Learning: Making the Transition." Reprinted with permission from Learning & Leading with Technology, vol. 23 no. 7, pp. 25-30, copyright (c) 1996, ISTE (International Society for Technology in Education) at http://www.educause.edu/nlii/articles/dede.html
10. Wright, T. Interview with Chris Dede. Syllabus Magazine. June 2002. http://www.syllabus.com/syllabusmagazine/article.asp?id=6388
11. Brown, J.S. Growing Up Digital:How the Web Changes Work, Education, and the Ways People Learn. USDLA Journal. Vol 16: No. 2.

February 2002. http://www.usdla.org/html/journal/FEB02_Issue/article01.html

12. Chickering, A., Ehrmann, S. "Implementing the Seven Principles: Technology as Lever." http://www.aahe.org/ehrmann.htm

13. Hartman, J., Dziuban, C., Moskal, P. "Faculty Satisfaction in ALNs: A Dependent or Independent Variable?" In *Online Education, Volume 1*. Needham, MA: Sloan-C, 2000. *Journal of Asynchronous Learning Networks*. JALN, Volume 4, Issue 2. September 2000. http://www.aln.org/alnweb/journal/jaln-volume4issue3.htm

14. Hiltz, R., Coppola, N., Rotter, N., Turoff, M. "Measuring the Importance of Collaborative Learning for the Effectiveness of ALN: A Multi Measure, Multi-Method Approach." In *Online Education, Volume 1*. Needham, MA: Sloan-C, 2000. *Journal of Asynchronous Learning Networks*. JALN, Volume 4, Issue 2. September 2000. http://www.aln.org/alnweb/journal/jaln-vol4issue2.htm

15. Fredericksen, E., Pickett, A., Shea, P., Pelz, W., Swan, K. "Student Satisfaction and Perceived Learning with Online Courses: Principles and Examples from the SUNY Learning Network." In *Online Education, Volume 1*. Needham, MA: Sloan-C, 2002. *Journal of Asynchronous Learning Networks*. JALN, Volume 4, Issue 2. September 2000. http://www.aln.org/alnweb/journal/jaln-volume4issue3.htm

16. Keeton, M.T., Scheckley, B.G, Krecji-Griggs, J. *Effectiveness and Efficiency in Higher Education for Adults.* Council on Adult and Experiential Learning. Chicago: Kendall-Hunt, 2002.

17. Shea, P., Swan, K., Fredericksen, E., Pickett, A. "Student Satisfaction and Reported Learning in the SUNY Learning Network." In *Elements of Quality Online Education: Volume 3 in the ™ Series.* Needham, MA: Sloan-C, 2002.

18. Islam, K. Is E-learning Floundering? Identifying shortcomings and preparing for success. E-learning Magazine. May 1, 2002. http://www.elearningmag.com/elearning/article/articleDetail.jsp?id=18563

19. Twigg, C. "Innovations in Online Learning: Moving Beyond No Significant Difference." The Pew Learning and Technology Program. December 2000. http://www.center.rpi.edu/PewSym/mono4.html

20. Trippe, T. "Student Satisfaction at the University of Phoenix Online Campus." In *Elements of Quality Online Education: Volume 3 in the ™ Series*. Needham, MA: Sloan-C, 2002.

21. Arvan, L. The Excelets Page. http://edtech3.cet.uiuc.edu/l-arvan/ExceletsWeb/ExceletsHome.htm

22. Kashy, E., Thoennessen, M., Alberti, G., Tsai, Y. "Implementing a Large On-Campus ALN: Faculty Perspective." Online Education, Volume 1. Needham, MA: Sloan-C, 2000. *Journal of Asynchronous Learning Networks*. JALN, Volume 4, Issue 2. September 2000. http://www.aln.org/alnweb/journal/jaln-volume4issue3.htm

Appendix D: References (by section)

23. Serendip. http://serendip.brynmawr.edu
24. University of Massachusetts Center for Information Technology and Dispute Resolution. http://www.ombuds.org/course2001/odr101.htm
25. DiBiase, D. "Using e-Portfolios at Penn State to Enhance Student Learning: Status, Prospects, and Strategies." February 16, 2002. http://www.e-education.psu.edu/portfolios/e-port_report.shtml
26. Moseley, B. "Increasing the Effectiveness of Online Education through Personalization." http://www.bmoseley.com/research/arp/Default.asp
27. Bransford, J., Brown, A. L., Cocking, R.R., Eds. *How People Learn: Brain, Mind, Experience, and School: Expanded Edition*. Washington, D.C.: National Academy Press, 2000. http://www.nap.edu/books/0309070368/html/
28. Miller, G. Excerpts from Sloan-C™ listserv emails dated January 10 and January 17, 2002.
29. Pimentel, J. "Design of Net-learning Systems Based on Experiential Learning." *Journal of Asynchronous Learning Networks*. JALN, Volume 3, Issue 2. November 1999. http://www.aln.org/alnweb/journal/Vol3_issue2/pimentel.htm
30. Swan, K. "Immediacy, Social Presence, Asynchronous Discussion." In *Elements of Quality Online Education: Volume 3 in the ™ Series*. Needham, MA: Sloan-C, 2002.
31. The Sloan Consortium Effective Practices: http://www.sloan-c.org/effectivepractices
32. Campos, M., Laferrière, T., Harasim, L. "The Post-Secondary Networked Classroom: Renewal of Teaching Practices and Social Interaction." *Journal of Asynchronous Learning Networks*. JALN, Volume 5: Issue 2. http://www.aln.org/alnweb/journal/Vol5_Issue2
33. Blum, K. "Gender Differences in Asynchronous Learning in Higher Education: Learning Styles, Participation Barriers and Communication Patterns." *Journal of Asynchronous Learning Networks*. JALN, Volume 3, Issue 1. May 1999. http://aln.org/alnweb/journal/Vol3_issue1/blum.htm
34. Beaudin, B. "Keeping Online Asynchronous Discussions on Topic." *Journal of Asynchronous Learning Networks*. JALN, Volume 3: Issue 2. http://www.aln.org/alnweb/journal/Vol3_issue2
35. Turoff, M., Hiltz, S.R. "Effectively Managing Large Enrollment Courses: A Case Study." In *Online Education, Volume 2*. Needham, MA: Sloan-C, 2001.
36. Andriole, S. "Requirements-Driven ALN Course Design, Development, Delivery & Evaluation." *Journal of Asynchronous Learning Networks*. JALN, Volume 1, Issue 2. August 1997. http://www.aln.org/alnweb/journal/issue2/andriole.htm
37. Taylor, J. "Virtual Writing Forum With Don Murray and the National Writing Project in an Asynchronous Environment." *Journal of*

Asynchronous Learning Networks. JALN, Volume 5: Issue 1. June 2001. http://www.aln.org/alnweb/journal/Vol5_issue1/Taylor/Taylor.htm

38. Brown, R.E. "The Process of Building Community in Distance Learning Classes." *Journal of Asynchronous Learning Networks.* JALN, Volume 5: Issue 2. http://www.aln.org/alnweb/journal/Vol5_issue2

39. Vandergrift, K. "The Anatomy of a Distance Education Course: A Case Study Analysis." *Journal of Asynchronous Learning Networks.* JALN Volume 6: Issue 1. July 2002.

40. Rovai, A. "A Preliminary Look at Structural Differences in Sense of Classroom Community between Higher Education Traditional and ALN Courses/" JALN Volume 6, Issue 1 -July 2002.

41. Gold, S. "A Constructivist Approach to Online Training for Online Teachers." *Journal of Asynchronous Learning Networks.* JALN, Vol 5: Issue 1. http://www.aln.org/alnweb/journal/jaln-vol5_issue1.htm

42. The National Survey of Student Engagement. "The College Student Report: Effective Educational Practices, An Untapped Dimension of Quality." NSSE 2000. http://www.indiana.edu/~nsse/acrobat/report-2000.pdf

43. Staley, A., MacKenzie, N. "Enabling Curriculum Re-design Through Asynchronous Learning Networks." *Journal of Asynchronous Learning Networks.* JALN, Volume 4: Issue 1. http://www.aln.org/alnweb/jounral/Vol4_issue1/staleyMacKenzie.htm

44. Crumpton Curriculum Design Concept Map. http://www.lmu.uce.ac.uk/crumpton/curriculum-design.htm

45. McNaught, C. "Quality Assurance for Online Courses: Implementing Policy at RMIT." In *Assessment: The Technology Source.* January/February 2002. http://ts.mivu.org/default.asp?show=article&id=940

46. Moore, M. "Editorial: Is Distance Teaching More Work or Less?" *The American Journal of Distance Education.* Volume 14, Number 3, 2000. http://www.ajde.com/Contents/vol14_3.htm

47. Coppola, N., Hiltz, S. R., Rotter, N. "The Effective Digital Socrates: Developing Trust in Virtual Learning Communities." Presentation at the 6th Annual Sloan ALN Conference, November 2001. http://dce.ucf.edu/aln/sessions/htm

The Pillars: Cost Effectiveness

48. Carr, S. "Is Anyone Making Money on Distance Education?" *The Chronicle of Higher Education.* February 16, 2001.

49. Sloan-C™ Online Learning Enrollment Suvey: http://www.sloanconsortium.org/alnenrollments/showdata.cfm

50. Estabrook, L. "Rethinking Cost Benefit Models of Instruction." In *Elements of Quality Online Education: Volume 3 in the Sloan-C™ Series.* Needham, MA: Sloan-C, 2002.

Appendix D: References (by section)

51. Shea, P., Pelz, W., Fredericksen, E. and Pickett, A.M. "Online Teaching as a Catalyst for Classroom-Based Instructional Transformation." In *Elements of Quality Online Education: Volume 3 in the Sloan-C™ Series*. Needham, MA: Sloan-C, 2002.

52. Stokes, P., Evans, T. "After the Big Bang: Higher Education E-Learning Markets Get Set to Consolidate." Eduventures.com: October 2000. http://www.educventures.com/research/industry_research_resources/big_bang.cfm

53. World Lecture Hall: http://www.utexas.edu/world/lecture

54. Merlot: http://www.merlot.com

55. TLT Group: http://www.tltgroup.org

56. Centre for Curriculum, Transfer and Technology: http://www.c2t2.ca

57. ADEC Courseware Tools: http://www.adec.edu/courseware.html

58. Educause: http://www.educause.edu/ep/

59. Knowledge Media Lab: http://kml2.carnegiefoundation.org/gallery/index.html

60. Feldberg, J. "Five Insider Secrets to Designing and Developing EFFECTIVE Online Course in Record Time Without a Big Budget." Educational Pathways. January 2002. http://www.edpath.com

61. Gilbert, S. Low Threshold Applications. http://tc.unl.edu/cansorge/lowthreshold/

62. Eustis, J., McMillan, G. "Libraries Address the Challenges of Asynchronous Learning." *Journal of Asynchronous Learning Networks*. JALN, Volume 2, Issue 1, March 1998. http://www.aln.org/alnweb/jounral/vol2_issue1/eustis.htm

63. Collaborative Digital Reference Service, http://www.loc.gov/rr/digiref

64. The Internet Public Library: http://www.ipl.org

65. The Lincoln Library: http://lincoln.library.uiuc.edu:8000

66. Massachusetts Institute of Technology OpenCourseWare: http://web.mit.edu/ocw

67. Reid, I. "Beyond Models: Developing a University Model for Online Instruction." *Journal of Asynchronous Networks*. Volume 3, Issue 1 - May 1999. http://www.aln.org/alnweb/journal/Vol3_issue1/reid.htm

68. Bishop, T., SchWeber, C. "UMUC's Online MBA Program: A Case Study of Cost Effectiveness and the Implications for Large-scale Programs." In *Online Education, Volume 2*. Needham, MA: Sloan-C, 2001.

69. Hislop, G. "Operating Cost of an Online Degree Program." In *Online Education, Volume 2*. Needham, MA: Sloan-C, 2001.

70. Miller, G. "Penn State's World Campus: A Case Study in Achieving Cost Efficiencies in ALN." In Online *Education, Volume 2*. Needham, MA: Sloan-C, 2001.

71. Twigg, C. "Improving Learning and Reducing Costs: Redesigning Large-Enrollment Courses. The Pew Learning and Technology Program." July 1999. http://www.center.rpi.edu/PewSm/mono2.html

72. Moonen, J. "The Efficiency of Telelearning." *Journal of Asynchronous Learning Networks*. JALN, Volume 1, Issue 2. August 1997. http://www.aln.org/alnweb/journal/issue2/moonen.htm

73. Twigg, C. "Improving Learning and Reducing Costs: Redesigning Large-Enrollment Courses. The Pew Learning and Technology Program." July 1999. http://www.center.rpi.edu/PewSm/mono2.html

74. Bishop, T., SchWeber, C. "Linking Quality and Cost." In *Elements of Quality Online Education: Volume 3 in the Sloan-C™ Series*. Needham, MA: Sloan-C, 2002.

75. The Pew Grant Program in Course Redesign Course Planning Tool http://www.center.rpi.edu/PewGrant/Tool.html

76. The Centre for Curriculum, Transfer & Technology. Online Educational Delivery Applications: A Web Tool for Comparative Analysis. http://www.c2t2.ca/landonline

77. Morgan, B. Determining the Costs of Online Education. http://webpages.marshall.edu/~morgan16/onlinecosts

78. Jones, D. *Technology Costing Methodology Project*. WCET and WICHE, March 2001. http://www.wiche.edu/telecom/projects/tcm/TCM_Handbook_Final.pdf

79. American Council of Education. Academic Excellence and Cost Management National Awards Program: http://www.acenet.edu/about/programs/programs&analysis/policy&analysis/cost-awards/

80. The Mellon Foundation: "Cost Effective Uses of Technology in Teaching." http://www.ceutt.org/

81. National Association of College and University Business Officers. "Explaining College Costs: NACUBO's Methodology For Identifying The Costs of Delivering Undergraduate Education." http://www.nacubo.org/public_policy/cost_of_college/content.html

82. Rumble, G. "The Costs and Costing of Networked Learning." *Journal of Asynchronous Learning Networks*. JALN, Volume 5, Issue 2. September 2001. http://aln.org/alnweb/journal/Vol5_issue2/Rumble/Rumble.htm

83. Graves, W. "Free Trade in Higher Education: The Meta University." *Journal of Asynchronous Learning Networks*. Volume 1, Issue 1. http://www.aln.org/alnweb/journal/issue1/graves.htm

84. Twigg, C., Heterick, R. "It's Not How Fast You Run." *The Learning MarketSpace*. March 1, 2002. http://www.center.rpi.edu/LForum/LdfLM.html

The Pillars: Access

85. The National Center for Education Statistics report is available at http://www.nces.ed.gov

86. The Campus Computing Project. http://www.campuscomputing.net/

Appendix D: References (by section)

87. The Digital Divide Network. http://www.digitaldividenetwork.org/content/sections/index.cfm?key=2

88. Thompson, M., McGrath, J. "Using ALNs to Support a Complete Educational Experience." *Journal of Asynchronous Learning Networks.* JALN, Volume 3, Issue 2. November 1999. http://www.aln.org/alnweb/journal/jaln-vol3issue2.htm

89. The Centre for Curriculum, Transfer and Technology at http://www.c2t2.ca/landonline/ provides useful analyses of CMS features, including a checklist that begins with pedagogical features.

90. Bourne, J., Brodersen, A., Campbell, J., Dawant, M. Shiavi, R. "A Model of Online Learning Networks in Engineering Education." *Journal of Asynchronous Learning Networks.* JALN, Volume 1, Issue 1. March 1997. http://www.aln.org/alnweb/jounral/issue1/bourne.htm

91. Stokes, P. "CMS Users Still Waiting for the Killer App: Higher Education Institutions Seek Improved Support Services and Greater Integration from Leading Providers of Course Management Systems." Eduventures.com. February 2001. http://www.eduventures.com/research/industry_research_resources/cms_report.cfm

92. eArmyU. RFP for prospective partners at: http://www.earmyu.com/public/public_about-auao_become-a-partner.asp

93. de Castell, S., Bryson, M., Jenson, J. "Object Lessons: Towards an *Educational* Theory of Technology." *First Monday.* Volume 7, Number 1 - January 7 2002. http://www.firstmonday.dk/issues/issue7_1/index.html

94. Neal, L. "Predictions for 2002." ELearn Magazine. http://www.elearnmag.org/subpage/sub_page.cfm?article_pk=2901&page_number_nb=1&title=COLUMN

95. Granger, D. & Benke, M. "Supporting Learners at a Distance from Inquiry Through Completion." *Distance Learners in Higher Education: Institutional Responses for Quality Outcomes,* Campbell, C. editor. Gibson. Atwood Publishing, Madison, Wisconsin, 1998.

96. Sachs, D., Hale, N. "Pace University's Focus on Student Satisfaction With Student Services in Online Education." In *Elements of Quality Online Education: Volume 3 in the ™ Series.* Needham, MA: Sloan-C, 2002.

97. McGrath, J., Middleton, H., Crissman, T. "World Campus: Setting Standards in Student Services." In *Elements of Quality Online Education: Volume 3 in the Sloan-C™ Series.* Needham, MA: Sloan-C, 2002.

98. Thompson, M., McGrath, J. Using ALNs to Support a Complete Educational Experience. JALN, Volume 3: Issue 2, November 1999.

99. Southern Regional Electronic Board: http://www.evalutech.sreb.org/criteria/web.asp

100. Environmental Education and Training Partnership. EETAP: http://www-comdev.ag.ohio-state.edu/eetap/publications.htm

101. World Wide Web Consortium (W3C) guidelines: http://www.w3.org/WAI/Resources/#gl

Pillar Reference Manual

102. Bobby Approval: http://www.cast.org/bobby/
103. Krauth, B., Carbajal, J. Guide to Developing Online Student Services: http://www.wiche.edu/telecom/resources/publications/guide/guide.htm accessed 2/8/02
104. Advanced Distributed Learning Network: http://www.adlnet.org/home.cfm
105. Advance Distributed Learning Network Co Lab. http://www.wiadlcolab.org/
106. MIT Open Knowledge Initiative: http://web.mit.edu/oki/
107. IMS Global Learning Consortium, Inc. http://www.imsproject.org/aboutims.html

The Pillars: Faculty Satisfaction

108. Newman, F., Scurry, J. "Online Technology Pushes Pedagogy to the Forefront." *The Chronicle of Higher Education.* July 13, 2001. http://chronicle.com/weekly/v47/i44/44b00701.htm
109. Occupational Outlook Handbook: http://www.bls.gov/oco/ocos066.htm
110. *The Chronicle of Higher Education.* "Reliance on Part-Time Faculty Members and How They Are Treated, Selected Disciplines." December 2001. http://chronicle.com/weekly/v47/i14/14a01301.htm. Based on data from the American Historical Association: http://www.theaha.org/caw/index.htm
111. Bradburn, E. Distance Education Instruction by Postsecondary Faculty and Staff: Fall 1998. http://nces.ed.gov/pubsearch/pubsinfo.asp?pubid=2002155
112. Turgeon, A. "Introducing the Penn State World Campus through Certificate Program in Turfgrass Management and Geographic Information Systems." In *Online Education, Volume 1.* Needham, MA: Sloan-C, 2000. *Journal of Asynchronous Learning Networks.* JALN, Volume 4, Issue 3. September 2000. http://www.aln.org/alnweb/journal/Vol4_issue3/fs/turgeon/fs-turgeon.htm
113. Arvan, L. "An Introduction to Faculty Satisfaction." In *Online Education, Volume 1.* Needham, MA: Sloan-C, 2000. *Journal of Asynchronous Learning Networks.* JALN, Volume 4, Issue 3. September 2000. http://www.aln.org/alnweb/journal/jaln-vol4issue3.htm
114. Shapley, P. "On-line Education to Develop Complex Reasoning Skills in Organic Chemistry." *Journal of Asynchronous Learning Networks.* JALN, Volume 4, Issue 2. September 2000. http://www.aln.org/alnweb/journal/Vol4_issue2/le/shapley/LE-shapley.htm
115. Thaiupathump, C., Bourne, J., Campbell, O. "Intelligent Agents for Online Learning." *Journal of Asynchronous Learning Networks.* JALN, Volume 3, Issue 2. November 1999. http://www.aln.org/alnweb/journal/Vol3_issue2/Choon2.htm

Appendix D: References (by section)

116. Latchman, H.A. "Lectures on Demand in ALN: Enhancing the Online Learning Experience." *Journal of Asynchronous Learning Networks.* JALN, Volume 5, Issue 1. June 2001. http://www.aln.org/alnweb/journal/Vol5_issue1/Latchman/Latchman.htm

117. Campbell, O. "Factors In ALN Cost Effectiveness at BYU." In *Elements of Quality Online Education: Volume 3 in the Sloan-C™ Series.* Needham, MA: Sloan-C, 2002.

118. Hawisher, G., Pemberton, M. "Writing Across the Curriculum Encounters Asynchronous Learning Networks or WAC Meets Up With ALN." *Journal of Asynchronous Learning Networks.* JALN, Volume 1, Issue 1. March 1997. http://www.aln.org/alnweb/journal/issue1/hawisher.htm

119. Lynch, D. "Professors Should Embrace Technology." *The Chronicle of Higher Education.* January 18, 2002. http://chronicle.com/weekly/v48/i19/19b01501.htm

120. Jaffee, D. "Institutionalized Resistance To Asynchronous Learning Networks." Journal of Asynchronous Learning Networks. JALN, Volume 2, Issue 2. September 98. http://www.aln.org/alnweb/journal/vol2_issue2/jaffee.htm

121. Young, J. "Ever So Slowly, Colleges Start to Count Work With Technology in Tenure Decisions." *The Chronicle of Higher Education.* February 22, 2002.

122. Thompson, M. "Faculty Satisfaction in Penn State's World Campus." In *Online Education, Volume 2.* Needham, MA: Sloan-C, 2001.

123. Rockwell, S., Schauer, J., Fritz, S., Marx D. "Incentives and Obstacles Influencing Higher Education Faculty and Administrators to Teach Via Distance." *Online Journal of Distance Learning Administration.* Volume 2, Number 3. Winter1999. http://www.westga.edu/~distance/rockwell24.html

124. Green, K. *The Chronicle of Higher Education.* "Colloquy Live" discussion on Working with Technology and Winning Tenure. February 20, 2002. http://chronicle.com/colloquylive/2002/02/tenure/chat.php3

125. American Association for History and Computing. Guidelines for Evaluating Digital Media Activities in Tenure, Review, and Promotion. October 2001. http://www.theaahc.org/tenure_guidelines.htm

126. Bourne, J. "Net-Learning*: Strategies for On-Campus and Off-Campus Network-enabled Learning." *Journal of Asynchronous Learning Networks.* JALN, Volume 2, Issue 2. September 98. http://www.aln.org/alnweb/journal/vol2_issue2/bourne2.htm

127. University of Maryland Center for Intellectual Property. http://www.umuc.edu/distance/odell/cip/workshop_ipacademia/faq.html

128. Maryland Online. http://www.mdfaconline.org/

129. Schroeder, R. http://people.uis.edu/rschr1/bloggerinfo.html

130. Graham, C., Cagiltay, K., Lim, B., Craner, J. and Duffy, T. "Seven Principles of Effective Teaching: A Practical Lens for Evaluating Online

Courses." March/April 2001. http://horizon.unc.edu/TS/default.asp?show=article&id=839 and results: http://crlt.indiana.edu/publications/crlt00-13.pdf

131. "Report of the University of Illinois Teaching at an Internet Distance Seminar, December, 1999." http://www.vpaa.uillinois.edu/tid/report/

132. American Association of University Professors. "Statement on Distance Education." 1999. http://www.aaup.org/govrel/distlern/spcdistn.htm

133. Young, J. "Professor Says Distance Education Will Flop Unless Universities Revamp Themselves." *The Chronicle of Higher Education.* June 29, 2001.

134. Berg, G. "Early Patterns of Faculty Compensation for Developing and Teaching Distance Learning Courses." *Journal of Asynchronous Learning Networks.* JALN, Volume 4, Issue 1. June 2000. http://www.aln.org/alnweb/journal/Vol4_issue1/berg.htm

The Pillars: Student Satisfaction

135. Montessori, M. *The Discovery of the Child.* Oxford, England, Clio Press: 1989. "Actually, [the teacher] will learn from the child himself the ways and means to his own education, that is, [the teacher] will learn from the child himself how to perfect himself as a teacher." http://www.moteaco.com/clio/discovery.pdf

136. Rossman, M. "Successful Online Teaching Using An Asynchronous Learner Discussion Forum." *Journal of Asynchronous Learning Networks.* JALN, Volume 3, Issue 2. November 1999. http://www.aln.org/alnweb/journal/Vol3_issue2/Rossman.htm

137. DiPaolo, A. Online Education: "The Rise of a New Educational Industry." January 24, 2001. http://scpd.stanford.edu/SCPD/js/brandingFrame/externalURL.htm

138. National Center for Education Statistics. "2001, Condition of Education: Participation in Adult Learning." http://nces.ed.gov/

139. National Center for Public Policy and Higher Education. "Measuring Up 2000: The State-by-State Report Card for Higher Education." http://measuringup2000.highereducation.org/nationalpicture.htm

140. Carr, S. "As Distance Education Comes of Age, the Challenge Is Keeping the Students." *The Chronicle of Higher Education.* February 11, 2000. http://chronicle.com/free/v46/i23/23a00101.htm

141. Dutton, J., Dutton, M. and Perry, J. 'How Do Online Students Differ From Lecture Students?" *Journal of Asynchronous Learning Networks.* JALN Volume 6, Issue 1: July 2002.

142. Schrum, L. and Hong, S. "Dimensions and Strategies for Online Success: Voices from Experienced Educators." *Journal of Asynchronous Learning Networks.* JALN, Volume 6: Issue 1. July 2002.

143. "Online Learning: Is It for Me?" http://www.monroecc.edu/depts/distlearn/minicrs/10mythsindex.htm

144. Sener, J., Stover, M. ""Integrating ALN into an Independent Study Distance Education Program: NVCC Case Studies." In *Online Education, Volume 1*. Needham, MA: Sloan-C, 2000. *Journal of Asynchronous Learning Networks*. JALN, Volume 4, Issue 3. September 2000. . http://www.aln.org/alnweb/journal/jaln-vol4issue3.htm

145. Tello S. An Analysis of the Relationship Between Instructional Interaction and Student Persistence in Online Education. 2002. http://frontpage.uml.edu/faculty/stello/publications.htm

146. Sloan-C™ listserv discussion in June 2000, quoted by permission.

147. McFarlane, F., Baars, A., Stevens, B., Warn, M. "Effectiveness of Distance Education as a Means for Graduate Education - a Study of Two Student Groups." Nd. http://www.distance-educator.com/dailynews/mcfarland_print.htm

148. Twigg, C. "Quality Assurance for Whom? Providers and Consumers in Today's Distributed Learning Environment." December, 2000. http://www.center.rpi.edu/PewSym/mono3.html

149. Duderstadt, J. "The Future of the University in an Age of Knowledge." *Journal of Asynchronous Learning Networks*. JALN, Volume 1, Issue 2. August 1997. http://www.aln.org/alnweb/journal/issue2/duderstadt.htm

150. Eaton, J. "Core Academic Values, Quality, and Regional Accreditation: The Challenge of Distance Learning." Council for Higher Education Accreditation. Washington, DC. 2000. http://www.chea.org/Research/core-values.cfm

151. The Boyer Commission on Educating Undergraduates in the Research University. "Reinventing Undergraduate Education: A Blueprint for America's Research Universities."

Index

A

Academic Excellence and Cost Management
  national awards for 24
academic freedom
  faculty resistance and 37
access
  affordable 26
  benefits of wider 26
  defined 56
  educational, increased 25
  goals of 56
  key practice areas for 57
  metrics for 74
  practices of 74
  principles of 57
  quality of, assessing 2
  quick reference to 69
  student satisfaction and 26
  support for 56, 57
  unreliable 57
access, Internet 26
accessbility guidelines 32
accessibility
  Bobby and 32
accreditation reviews 50
adjunct faculty
  increase in 34, 42
Advanced Distributed Learning initiative 32
affordable access 26
agentive course work 10
agentive learning 16, 20
agents, intelligent 47
Al-harthi, Mohamad 71
Alexander the Great 1
allocation, faculty time 39
ALN. *See* asynchronous learning networks
American Association for Higher Education 8
American Association for History and Computing 38
American Council of Education 6
American Council of Education Center for Policy An 24
American Distance Education Consortium 6, 22
American Political Science Association 38
Andriole, Steve 14
androgogical curricula 20
androgogy
  defined 20
anonymity, student feelings of 49
Aquinas, Thomas 7
Aristotle 1
Arvan, Lanny 10
assessment
  online teaching and classroom teaching 22
asynchronous learning networks 2
  defined 2
asynchronous online programs 6
attrition, student. *See also* retention, student
  busy schedules and 44
  institutional setting and 45
  professional obligations and 47
  reasons for 44
  technology and 44
  tuition and 46

B

Baker, Amy 71
Barnes, Mary 71
barriers
  dispositional 14
  institutional 14
  situational 14
Beaudin, Bart 14
behaviorist learning styles 16
benefits, measuring long-term 47

benefits of online teaching 34
Benke, M. 30
Benke, Meg 71
Berg, G. 41
Bishop, T. 23
Bishop, Tana 24
blended delivery offerings 43
Blum, K. 14
Bobby accessbility approval 32
Bourne, John 39, 71
Boyer Commission 51
Brigham Young University 35, 47
Brown, John Seely 8
Brown, Judy 71
Brown, Ruth 14
Bryn Mawr 11
Bundy, Dennis 71
business of education
   defined 5

C

California, University of. *See*
   University of California
Campbell, Olin 47
Campos, M. 13
Campus Computing Project 36, 38
Campus Computing Report 26
CAPA
   student problems and 10
capacity management 6
Capella University 43
Carpenter, Jeff 71
Center for Professional Development 43
Center for Research on Learning and Technology 40
Centre for Curriculum, Transfer, and Technology 22, 24
Chaloux, Bruce 71
Chapman, Suzette 71
Chickering, A. 8
Chronicle of Higher Education 21
class projects
   movie trailers and 11

PowerPoint and 11
classroom as sacred space 37
classroom teaching
   online teaching and 21
CMS. *See* course management systems
Cochrane, Paul 71
cognitive learning styles 16
Collaborative Digital Reference Service 22
collaborative learning 20
collegiality, enhancing 40
Commerce Department, United States 26
community
   meaning of 15
community building 14
   matrix for 14
consciousness, learner 12
constructivist learning 20
constructivist learning styles 16
consumer learning products 50
consumers, students as 59
continuous quality improvement 5, 23
   adoption in educational institutions 5
   business considerations vs. academic consideration 5
   precepts of 5
Coppola, N. 20
cost
   direct and indirect 25
   identifying 25
   impact and 24
   quality and 24
cost effectiveness
   comparative value and 20
   defined 55
   goals of 20, 55
   key practice areas for 56
   metrics for 55, 73
   practices of 73
   principles of 56
   quality and 20

quality indicators and 24
quality of, assessing 2
quick reference to 69
school profiles of 25
sharing strategies 22
cost projection 23
cost studies 25
course design 19
  HTML editors and 22
course designers 22
course efficacy 22
course management systems 24, 26
  decision factors for 26
  eArmyU and 27
  effects of 30
  objections to 30
  open-source 30
  percentile use of 36
  price of 26
course work, agentive 10
CQI. *See* continuous quality improvement
Crocker, Linda 71
Crumpton 17
cultures
  online learning and 11
curriculum design concepts 16
customers, students as 44

D

Daig, Bart 71
Darling, Donna 71
Davis, Sherri 71
Dawant, Martine 71
Deckelbaum, Howard 45
Dede, Chris 7, 41
demand, faculty
  projected growth for 34
design concepts, curriculum 16
design, course 19
  HTML editors and 22
designers, instructional 41
designers, course 22

DiBiase, David 11
digital divide 26
DiPaolo, Anthony 43, 44
divide, digital 26
document length
  scrolling and 18
Drexel University 47
Dutton, J. 44

E

eArmyU 27
  course management systems and 27
Educational Pathways Newsletter 22
educational technologists 41
Educause 22
Eduventures 26
effectiveness. *See* cost effectiveness
effectiveness, faculty
  development of 40
efficacy, course 22
Ehrmann, S. 8
Einstein, Albert 7
electricity, discovery of 12
emotional support 20
enrollment increases, dobule-digit 21
e-portfolios 11
e-publishing
  libraries and 22
Estabrook, L. 21
Estler, Don 71
evaluation policies, faculty 59
evaluations
  course 22
Excel models
  quantitative concepts and 10
Extended Learning Institute 46

F

face-to-face interaction 37
face-to-face learning

faculty - Instructional

online learning vs. 7
faculty, adjunct
  increase in 42
  increasing in 34
faculty demand
  projected growth for 34
faculty effectiveness
  development of 40
faculty resistance. *See* resistance, faculty
  tenure and 37
faculty review guidelines 38
faculty satisfaction. *See* satisfaction, faculty
faculty time allocation 39
Fairbanks, Andrew 71
feedback, automating 35
Feldberg, Jeffrey 22
Feldstein, Michael 30
Fife, Kathryn 71
first online programs 1
five pillars 2
  effectiveness of 3
  goals of 2, 5
  interdependence of 2, 53
flexibility
  online learning and 11
Florida, University of. *See* University of Florida
Florida, University of Central. *See* University of Central Florida
Frank, Linda 71
freedom, academic
  faculty resistance and 37

G

Galvin, Christopher 44
Gamson 8
gap analyses 6
Geith, C. 30
gender
  learning style and 14
Gilbert, Steve 22
Goldstein, Marci 71

Gould, Jay 71
Granger, D. 30
Graves, William 25
"growing up digital" 8
growth industry
  online education as 5

H

Harasim, L. 13, 48
Hartman, Laird 71
Herkimer County Community College 36, 45
Higher Education Research Institute 36
Hiltz, R. 7
Hiltz, S.R. 20
Hinrichs, Randy J. 33
Hislop, Gregory 23, 47, 81
holistic principles, guiding 1
Hong, S. 44
Hovis, Tricia 71
HTML editors
  course design and 22
hypertext
  overuse of 18

I

ice-breaking activities 17
Illinois, University of. *See* University of Illinois
Indiana University 40
individualize drelationships, maintaining 10
Industrial Revolution 7
information age 19
information society 12
Information Technologies Institute 45
Institute for Higher Education/NEA Benchmarks 6
institutional mission 6
institutional reputation 7
instructional designers 41
Instructional Practices Inventory 9

intellectual property 23, 40, 58
intelligent agents 47
interaction, learning
   four kinds of 13
interaction, peer-to-peer 13
interaction, vicarious 13
interactive multimedia 49
Internet
   access 26
   usage 26
Internet Public Library 22
interoperability, institutional 33
Islam, Kaliym 10, 20
isolation, student feelings of 49

J

Johnson, Susan 71
Johnstone, Sally 71
Jones, Dennis 24
Journal of Asynchronous Learning
   Networks 3, 35

K

Kashy, Ed 10
Keeton, M.T. 8, 9
Kenneth Green 38
Kick, Linda 71
Kidwell, Jill 71
Kime, Steve 71
Kletzel, June 71
knowledge, age of 50
Knowledge Media Lab 22
Krecji-Griggs, J. 8, 9

L

Laferrière, T. 13
Lafferty, Vincent 71
Leahy, Meredyth A. 71
learning
   vitalness of 12
learning effectiveness
   assessing 2
   defined 54

goals of 54
key practice areas for 54
metrics for 54, 72
pedagogy and 54
practices of 72
principles of 54
quick reference to 69
learning interaction
   four kinds of 13
learning styles 16, 22
   behaviorist 16
   cognitive 16
   constructivist 16
   gender and 14
   online learning and 10
legacies of knowledge 19
Legacy Cycle 19
legacy of higher education 50
Levin, Sandy 46
libraries
   Collaborative Digital Reference
     Service 22
   e-publishing ventures 22
   Internet Public Library 22
   restructuring in 22
lifelong learning 44
Lincoln, Abraham 7
Lincoln Library 22
literacy
   navigation and 8
long-term benefits, measuring 47
low threshold applications 22
LTA. *See* low threshold applications
Lynch, Diane 36

M

MacKenzie, N. 16
management systems, course
   24, 26. *See* course management systems
Marshall University 24
Martini, Louis 71
Maryland Online 40

Massachusetts - online

Massachusetts Institute of Technology 22
Massachusetts Open Knowledge Initiative 33
Mayadas, Frank 1, 2, 20, 71
McFarley, Jr., George 71
McGrath, Jean 31
McMichael, Jim 71
Meine, Manfred 71
Mellon Foundation Initiative on Cost Effective Use 24
Merlot 22
metrics
  cost effectiveness and 55
  learning effectiveness and 54
  showing progress with 3
  student satisfaction and 59
Michigan State University 10, 35
Microsoft's Learning Sciences and Technology 33
Miller, Gary 12, 71
Mills, Karen 71
mission, institutional 6
MIT. *See* Massachusetts Institute of Technology
moderator, instructor as 36
Modern Language Association 38
Moloney, Jacqueline 45
Monroe Community College 45
Moore, Janet 71
Moore, Michael 19, 42, 71
Morgan, Brian 24
Moseley, Bill 11
Motorola 44
movie trailers
  class projects and 11
multimedia, interactive 49
Murray, Don 14

N

NACUBO. *See* National Association of College and University Bus
National Association of College and University Bus 25
National Center for Education 34
National Center for Education Statistics 44
National Center for Educational Statistics 26
National Center for Higher Education Management Sy 24
National Center for Public Policy and Higher Educa 44
National Survey of Student Engagement 42
National Writing Project 14
navigation and literacy 8
New Jersey Institute of Technology 8
New York, State University of. *See* State University of New York
New York University 45
Newman, F. 33
norms and practices
  development of 42
Northern Virginia Community College 46

O

Oakley, Burks 46, 71
Oblinger, Diana 71
Ohio State University Environmental Education and 32
one-to-one instruction 1
online learning
  face-to-face learning, vs. 7
  flexibility in 11
  learning styles and 10
  personal preference and 10
  potential of 7, 11
  push and pull of 8
online pedagogy
  features of 12
  institutional pedagogy and 21
online programs
  first 1
online teaching

classroom teaching and 21
open-source e-learning platforms 30
options, evaluating learning 50
ownership, course content 23, 41

P

pedagogy
   features of online 12
   learning effectiveness and 54
   online and institutional 21
peer review 19
peer-to-peer interaction
   debate about 13
peer-to-peer learning 26
Pelz, William 45
Penn State 11, 23, 35, 40
   World Campus
      12, 23, 31, 35, 40, 41
Pepperdine 11
personal connections, making 11
personal preference
   online learning and 10
personalize learning 11
personalizing instruction 10
Pew Center for Academic Transformation 10
Pew Learning and Technology Program 24
Pew Monograph 23, 49
Philip of Macedonia 1
Phoenix, University of. *See* University of Phoenix
Pimentel, J. 13
Plato 1, 12
Poley, Janet 71
portals, learning
   evolution of 32
Porter, Cyndi Wilson 71
potential of online learning 7, 11
PowerPoint
   class projects and 11
PricewaterhouseCoopers 27
printing and education 1

printing press, invention of 12
Prisoner's Dilemma
   problem solving and 11
products, consumer learning 50
programmers 41
projecting costs 23
property, intellectual 23, 40, 58
purchasing power
   influence of 50
push and pull of online learning 8

Q

quality
   cost and 24
   defined 6
   institutional commitment to 55
quality framework
   commenting on 53
   purpose of 51
quality in online learning 1
quality online education
   guidelines for 6
Quinlan, Marjorie 71

R

Ramanujan, Srinivasa 7
Ramirez, Alex 71
Reeve, Kevin 71
reputation, institutional 7
resistance, faculty 36
   academic freedom and 37
   commercial interest and 41
   commercialization and 42
   content ownership and 41
   deprofessionalization and 42
   increased workload and 38
   reasons for 37
   technical skills and 38
   tenure and 37
   time requirements and 38
resources of online learning 54
retention, faculty 58
retention, long-term 11
retention, online course

support services and 45
retention, student 21. *See also* attrition, student
  flexibility and 46
  predicting 46
  quality improvement approach to 47
review guidelines, faculty 38
RMIT. *See* Royal Melbourne Institute of Technology
Robinson, Lynn 71
Rockwell, S. 38
Rogich, Michael 71
Rossman, M. 43
Rotter, N. 20
Rovai, A. 15
Royal Melbourne Institute of Technology 19
Rumble, Greville 25
Runyon, Darla 71

S

Saba 41
sacred space, classroom as 37
satisfaction, faculty 36
  assessing 2
  defined 33, 58
  factors of 58
  key practice areas for 58
  metrics for 75
  practices of 75
  principles of 58
  quick reference to 70
  reward systems and 58
satisfaction, student 42. *See* satisfaction, student
  assessing 2
  attrition and 44
  benchmarks for 43
  defined 42, 59
  goals of 59
  interaction and 59
  key practice areas for 59
  long-term benefits and 47

metrics for 59, 76
practices of 76
principles of 60
quick reference to 70
saw, sharpening the metaphor of 53
Scheckley, B.G. 8, 9
Schroeder, Ray 40
Schrum, L. 44
SchWeber, C. 23
SCORM. *See* Shareable Content Object Reference Model
Scott, Kimberly 71
scrolling
  document length and 18
Scurry, J. 33
Seaman, Jeff 71
Sener, John 32, 46, 71
Serendip 11
Shareable Content Object Reference Model 30, 32
Sheldon, Jennifer 71
shyness
  online learning and 15
Sloan Consortium 3, 6
Sloan Foundation 1, 2
Sloan-C 13, 24, 32, 42, 45
Snead, Kathy 71
social connections, making 11
social presence 13
socioeconomic precepts
  college education and 25
Southern Regional Board 32, 33
Southern Regional Electronic Campus 6
Staley, A. 16
Stanford University 43
State University of New York 8, 9, 35, 39
State University of New York Learning Network 17, 21, 35, 39, 49
Stemmer, Paul 71
Stevens, Kerri 71
Stoskopf, Dian 71

student feedback 31
students. See also retention, student; satisfaction, student
  anonymity, feelings of 49
  consumers, as 59
  customers, as 44
  expectations of 43, 46, 48
  isolation, feelings of 49
  needs of 49
  shoppers, as sophisticated 30
students as customers 42
subject matter specialists 41
support, emotional 20
support services 30
  ethics and 31
  types of 31
Swan, K. 13

T

Taylor, Joan 14
teaching
  online and classroom 21
technologists, educational 41
Technology Costing Methodology 24
technology, influence of 8
Tello, S. 45
Thoennessen, Michael 10
Thompson, M. 41
Thompson, Melody 42, 71
time
  effort and 20
  sacred commodity, as 19
TLT 22
total quality management 5
  precepts of 5
TQM. See total quality management
traditional paradigms of learning 7
  alma mater 7
  master/apprentice 7
  novice/expert 7
  parent/child 7
  professor/pupil 7
  sage/disciple 7
  teacher/learner 7
Trippe, Tony 71
trust
  establishing 20
  online learning and 15
  two dimensions of 15
Turoff, Murray 14

U

United States Commerce Department 26
University of Amherst 11
University of California 35
University of California as Los Angeles 37
University of Central Florida 8, 34
University of Florida 35
University of Illinois 10, 35, 40, 46
  Graduate School of Library and Information Science 21
University of Illinois-Urbana Champaign 46
University of Maryland 23, 24, 40
University of Massachusetts at Lowell 45
University of Phoenix 10, 39, 40

V

Valentine, Hank 71
van Zyl, Henry 71
Vanderbilt University 35
Vandergrift, K. 15
vicarious interaction 13
Vignare, K. 30
virtual networks 40
visual learners 10
vitalness of learning 12
Von Holzen, Roger 71

W

W3C. See World Wide Web

Consortium
WCET. *See* Western Cooperative for Educational Telecommunicat
Western Cooperative for Educational Telecommunicat
    6, 32, 81
White, David 71
Whittum, Terry 71
World Campus. *See* Penn State
World Lecture Hall 22
World Wide Web Consortium 32
Writing Across the Curriculum
    14, 35

Z

Zedlar, Stephanie 71